Ms. B...

Thank you for your love and constant support. You always remind me that "there are no limits". Many thanks... can't say it enough!

2018

PATHWAY
PURP to OSE

Find It.
Follow It.
Fulfill It.

ERICKA SALLEE

Sunny House Press

ISBN-13: 978-1719256209

ISBN-10: 1719256209

To my daughter Erin and my son Walter K, always dream big, work to make your dreams come true and know that all things are possible. I love you with all my heart. You are my "why."

God, thank you!

CONTENTS

Introduction ix

Chapter 1   Birthing the Baby 1

Chapter 2   Stagnation 7

Chapter 3   What Would You Do for Free 15

Chapter 4   Eyesight vs. Vision 25

Chapter 5   Planning and Patience 31

Chapter 6   Past Tense 41

Chapter 7   No Strangers on the Journey 61

Chapter 8   Gratitude 77

Chapter 9   Keep Pushing 87

Acknowledgements 99

About the Author 101

INTRODUCTION

I n 2007, I was sitting in my bedroom about to do my hair. At that time, I had written several iterations of my business plan to open a day spa, so I was feeling tremendous excitement about becoming an entrepreneur. While under the hair dryer, it hit me, "I should write a book!" Actually, I never imagined myself as an author but as I was writing my business plan I was learning so much about the process and discovering myself that I realized I had something to say that I wanted others to hear. Then, I was focusing on writing about how I received insight to open the spa and my philosophy on good health, which I believe is determined by three key components: what we think (our mind), how we look and feel (our body) and our guiding center (our spirit). I immediately created an outline and began organizing my thoughts around my newfound philosophy. I was on a roll, at least for a while.

But then I put down my pen and paper. I used to say, "life got in the way" and prevented me from writing because other things became my priority. The truth is that I had more to learn about myself and my purpose in the classroom we call life. What I started writing years ago is only a piece of what ended up on these pages.

So, let's talk about what this book is about. Let's talk about Purpose.

What I know for sure is that each of us has been created for a purpose, with gifts to give to the world. When we live our lives on purpose, we are more fulfilled and have a sense of well-being that is sometimes unexplainable. What does it mean to live your life on purpose? To live on purpose means you have a passion and commitment to do or be something of substance. You're creating a life that brings you joy, peace and abundance in your health, finances, creativity, energy, and relationships. More importantly, you're sharing all this goodness with others.

When I blew the dust off the book and started writing again, I didn't have money in a special account to fund this project. I had no idea how it was all going to come together. In the past this would have been the excuse I would have given myself to not move forward and finish. I remember that sinking feeling in the pit of my belly when I signed the contract with my editor and publisher, DeBora M. Ricks. I was at a conference in Atlanta. I decided that this time I wasn't going to quit. So, I made my way to the hotel's business center and signed, scanned and emailed the contract to her. I remember it like it was yesterday.

I was excited that I had finally taken the step toward giving birth to this book, but I was also nervous and uncertain. What in the world did I just do? Was I crazy? Was I ready? These were the questions that would normally cause me not to take that leap forward. Well, I guess I was ready because you are now reading my book! This journey reminds me that all things are possible when we embrace the fear and lean in anyway.

As I've taken this journey to living my purpose, there are some basic principles and practices that have resonated with me. In this book I'll show you how to find and know your purpose, how to follow it once you discover what it is, and how to fulfill it so that others are abundantly blessed.

This book will also show you the threads that I've woven together to help bring clarity to my purpose. I am grateful to DeBora for pushing and prodding me to expand beyond my comfort zone. Finally, it is my wish that this book will be the doorway for you to discover something about yourself that will stretch and guide you to your divine purpose, and once you're there, help you confidently walk in it.

CHAPTER 1

Birthing the Baby

*You are pregnant with possibilities! Give
birth now and be powerful.*
– Anyale Sam Chiyson

Everyone knows something about pregnancy, men and women alike. As a woman, whether you have physically given birth or not you've heard your share of stories about bringing human life into the world. Creation is a miracle, wouldn't you agree? It starts with the amazing act of fertilization, when two forces come together to make one being. During the early stages a woman may not even know she's pregnant, so she goes on with her daily routine until her body gives her signs like a missed period, tender breasts or something she eats makes her sick. When a woman discovers she's pregnant, she experiences any number of emotions. There could be fear, anxiety, joy, anticipation, and excitement. There might even be shock, which was what I felt when I found out that I was pregnant with my second child.

After my husband, Walter, and I had our daughter Erin, we tried having another child. After a while, we sadly concluded that it just wasn't going to happen for us. So, imagine the utter surprise when, nine years after Erin was born, I discovered I was pregnant again! That we'd just gotten rid of all Erin's baby stuff made this discovery even more interesting. But there's a feeling beyond shock and awe that comes over a newly pregnant woman that is unexplainable.

Especially for first-timers, the notion of parenthood may be frightening. After all, there's no instruction manual that accompanies motherhood. So, each woman must learn how to be a mother by trial and error. The woman who is happy to be expecting is elated to see her belly grow; she delights in the attention and care that she gets from others—doors held open, seats offered up, help with lifting heavy boxes.

And she prepares. She begins thinking about baby names, picks colors and a theme for the nursery, and packs her bag so that it is ready to grab and go when it's time to head to the hospital.

I, however, didn't have the luxury of packing my bag with Erin because I developed toxemia—also known as preeclampsia. That is, my blood pressure abruptly rose to dangerously high levels, putting my unborn and myself at risk. A trip to my doctor led to my going to the hospital that evening to prepare for delivery four weeks early. I was not prepared.

First, I had to call my husband at work to tell him that we were going to have a baby sooner than we thought. I can still hear the nervous excitement in his voice as he tried to process what I was saying. Then my mother-in-law and I had to make a quick run to the mall to get the things I would need in the hospital. The reality that I was about to become a mother was starting to sink in, along with all the angst that comes along with that. But the time had come. There was no more thinking, no more reading, no more planning. It was now time for action.

With my son, my husband and I had to plan the details of getting to the hospital. We lived more than 50 minutes from the hospital and, at the time,

I was working from home most of the week. My husband worked close to the hospital, so we had to really think about what would happen if I went into labor at home alone. Would he have to drive home to get me, then drive almost another hour to the hospital? Would I have to call an ambulance, which would take me to the closest hospital where I'd be tended to by unfamiliar medical staff? Who would pick up our daughter from the bus stop if we had to leave before she got home from school?

We were planning, and I was stressing over those details. But as it turned out my husband and I were both at home on the morning the contractions started. We monitored them through the day and didn't have to head to the hospital until our daughter was home from school. When it was time to go Erin and I sat in the back seat timing the contractions as my husband drove us to the hospital. I still have the piece of paper that she carefully wrote how far apart the contractions were. Talk about alignment!

All of the feel-good pregnancy stuff goes away when those labor pains kick in. Don't believe the hype that a woman forgets how painful childbirth was. Let me tell you, I have vivid memories of those pains. If you're a woman reading this book and you have given birth, I bet you do too! If you're a man, imagine someone kicking you in your testicles over and over and over again with a pair of steel-toe cowboy boots. Get the picture?

Carrying a life inside of you, one that is, at first, barely recognizable with no distinct characteristics, identity or form, feeling the flutters and stretching as it grows into a six, seven, eight or even larger pound baby is phenomenal.

When a baby has outgrown the womb, she will let you know she's ready to emerge. How? Mother will have contractions. Contractions indicate that the baby is getting in position. Contractions tell the soon-to-be-mom, doctors, and medical personnel that they must get ready too. By this time, that once cute little baby bump has grown so big that mom can barely see her swollen feet. Mother is ready for one thing and one thing only, she's ready to GET that baby OUT of her belly! And yet, the baby is in control. It won't emerge until *it's* ready.

Some contractions are just warning signs. They broadcast that the baby is getting into position to be born. It's not time to push just yet. In fact, if mother pushes too soon it could be detrimental to this new life. When those contractions get more intense, sometimes it feels like they're going to knock you off your feet. I remember walking the hall when I was in labor with my son, clutching the rail. My knees would buckle, because the contractions were so strong. I held onto the rail with one hand and my husband's arm with the other to keep from collapsing. He was feeling helpless because there was nothing he could do to ease my pain. With my daughter, I remember a sharp pressure in my lower back shooting around my body. I begged for more Epidural to ease my pain. Just when the pain became unbearable, my doctor instructed me to start pushing.

4

On the other side of pain is a blessing.

It was time to give birth to a new creation that started off so small and invisible to the outside world. I couldn't do it on my own, by myself, alone. Delivery—pushing the babies out—took coaching from doctors, nurses and my husband. I had to know exactly how to position myself, when to push and how to breathe. Not listening to the coaches could have meant harm to me and my babies. Through all the pain, all the moaning, groaning, sweating, cursing and exposure of every part of my body to anyone present in the delivery room, it finally happened. I felt the relief, heard the cries and saw the beauty of what took only moments to create, months to grow and hours to bring into the world. When I looked into the eyes of my babies the memory of the pain vanished. Actually, it's not that I forgot the pain but what I got for the pain was well worth what I went through.

Looking at those cute little faces and feeling the sheer joy of having brought life into the world reminds me that hard work pays off. I know for sure that during the pain of labor and delivery women have the power to tap into an inner strength that we seldom realize we have. The preparation and pain set us up to appreciate the joy of creation and motherhood.

WARNING SIGNS

This is not just about pregnancy in the physical sense. This is also about being pregnant with possibility and purpose. The Creator has given each of us gifts. These gifts are sometimes dormant, and they often stay that way as we move through life. School, work, family, church and a little fun become the norm.

Then something happens and we get a sign, much like the pregnant woman who notices that something is different with her body. The sign is not the same for everyone. For some, it's the passing of a loved one. For others it's the break up of a relationship (or start of a new one). For you, it might be getting fired or a niggling feeling that something is missing. Whatever it is, this thing, it tells you change is happening within you. This sign and discomfort are the nudge of purpose pushing from within.

Seldom do we recognize it, and "it" doesn't sound an alarm at first; rather it starts as a persistent whisper. You're frustrated with a situation that has lingered, or you're doing something that you've done for years only to find that it no longer serves you. It's recognizing that some in your circle are okay with the status quo or are not okay with their circumstances but don't think they can do anything to change them. But you want more. Some don't hear it because the distractions of life are so constant, consuming and loud that it's easy to ignore. Still, others *feel* something. It causes them to want to figure out what's in *their* soil and stirs their desire to water that fertile ground. We've all heard the phrase often enough, "I'm sick and tired of being sick and tired." That is, you've reached your limit; you're done with business as usual. You know something has to change. It's the beginning of the flow that can lead you straight into the flood of your purpose.

CHAPTER 2

Stagnation

*Stagnation is only a manifestation of the lack
of motivation of effort towards change.*
– Caleb Fairey

Stagnation means nothing is moving. There is no action. Thoughts and ideas have grown stale. For me, I knew I was stagnant when working in the corporate world was no longer fulfilling. I had achieved multiple levels of success with one company shortly after graduating from college. During the twenty years plus of my employment with this company I moved up the ranks. This was somewhat unusual because unlike my parents' and grandparents' generations, people in my era were job-hopping. So, to have that longevity was a major deal.

About fifteen years into my career I got the sign. Though I had great coworkers, had built lasting relationships, enjoyed working with some amazingly intelligent people, had learned a lot, received certifications, got bonuses and raises, I didn't feel good about what I was doing. Sure, I respected the job and the mission of the company; but I was not *feeling* it anymore. To be quite honest, I was in a technology-based environment where I never felt like I'd really mastered the various jobs that I held. Don't get me wrong, I met expectations and had good peer relationships; but I never reached the pinnacle of my profession as those around me expected me to. More significantly, I didn't have the desire to. I take nothing away from the company, the people, or the opportunities but I grew less interested in where I was. So the signs were there. The more I listened to the whispers the more I realized I was outgrowing the world I'd known for decades.

In 2008, when I was pregnant with my son, I really felt out of sorts in my career. I was excited about having my second child but was also uneasy. I know a lot of women who are stay-at-home moms, I, however, knew I was not one of them. Yet, I couldn't help but think how wonderful it would be if I could walk away from the corporate world. See, a few years prior to this I was inspired to start my own business, the details of which I'll share later in this book. But by this time I was really unfulfilled.

IMMACULATE CONCEPTION

The pregnancy hormones may have exacerbated my feelings of dissatisfaction; nonetheless, the feelings were strong. This, I believe, was the first time that I realized I was pregnant with more than the baby that was growing inside of me. I truly believe this was the first indication that I was spiritually pregnant, and that I was about to give birth to something that transcended anything I had ever conceived of for myself. I didn't have all the answers, but I knew there was something more that I was yearning for. I was having a hard time focusing on work because my mind was elsewhere. I was obsessed with what I wanted to do and be "when I grow up." I was a Project Manager, who just wasn't connected. Not to my team. Not to the work. On top of that I really didn't know much about project management in a techy world. Granted, some say it doesn't matter what field you're in project management is project management. I don't agree. I think it's easier when you speak the language and have some interest in what you're doing. I had neither. The project manager position was the next level up. I was competent and skilled in my previous positions so this move made sense.

So I went along to get along, as if I was in a trance. I did what everybody else was doing at the time. I went to work and maintained my home and family life.

> Restlessness is your spirit
> calling you to active duty.

Still, there was this feeling of uneasiness.

I think I was more restless with work than I was with my pregnancy. I was working on important projects, but the reality was that I was no more interested in them than I was in traveling to the moon. I was moving up but not growing, learning but not loving what I was doing. It was a tough place to be but I knew it was what I had to do in the meantime. I even took a professional certification exam that gave me special credentials because it was one of those silent expectations, not required but "nice to have because it makes you more marketable." So I went along. It was a noteworthy accomplishment, but I always felt that it was more for the culture than for me. Prior to that time in my life, I had never entertained being anywhere else but with that company, but as the intensity of dissatisfaction grew I started to think differently about my future. I became increasingly unenthused about going to work. Once there, it was a struggle and, again, it had less to do with the company and more to do with the picture I had of myself outside of the company. I was phasing myself out mentally and I know it showed in my work. Though I got it done, I wasn't the innovator or go-getter in that environment and I know that's what employers look for.

STIRRING MY SOUL

There were countless days when I would sit in meetings, and though I was in the room, I wasn't *really* there. My mind would be entertaining all the things I would do when I left work. What excited me was when my coworkers would come sit in my chair—the extra seat that most cubicles in my building had—and talk. They'd talk about their life, their ups and downs, their relationships, and their children. We'd laugh and sometimes cry. Those were the moments that were most invigorating to me because I felt like I was doing something that mattered in a way that work didn't. It was humbling to know they thought enough of me to share some of the most intimate details of their lives. And the embraces we would share were my way of solidifying a bond of confidence that I was keeping what they shared between us. Then I'd go back to the computer screen or to a meeting and reenter the world of make believe.

This went on for a few years. It was the delicate balance between being grateful for a job, having longevity in it, and desiring something more for the future. I felt increasingly unhappy, like I was stuck in a place that I had outgrown but wasn't quite ready to leave. So I remained stagnant in that environment. I know my lack of desire for my job was directly tied to my excitement about the new vision for myself that I was entertaining. Still, I needed to stay put because it just made sense to do so. I still needed to pay the mortgage, even as I planned for a new future.

> Sometimes change happens when
> you least expect it. And very
> often it's not on your terms.

Years after my son was born I was called into my manager's office for a conversation I hadn't anticipated. She was someone I respected a great deal and had a good working relationship with, so I'm sure the words she spoke were as uncomfortable for her to say as they were for me to hear. My manager told me I needed to start looking for another job, that my performance was not up to standard; consequently, I was no longer needed. Suddenly there was a lump in my throat. "You need to begin your job search immediately," she added, "or risk being placed on a performance improvement plan." I was in shock. I fought back the tears. I acted as if I was surprised but I knew my lack of enthusiasm had started to show. I'd been in denial up until then. Fear and uncertainty weighed me down. I thought I'd been successfully hiding my lack of interest. Clearly, I was mistaken. Not only was I feeling lackluster, but others were seeing it. Ugh! I had always planned to leave on my own terms. Funny how we are pushed into uncomfortable waters, like being pushed into a swimming pool before we're ready. The blessing was that I was given some time to look at other opportunities within the company—which, to this day, I still reflect on with gratitude.

This was a reality check for me. I certainly hadn't planned for this, but I knew it was a change that I needed, even if it wasn't how I envisioned it or had no clue as to what would happen next. Being pushed out of my comfort zone into taking the next step to work at another company until I could dive fully into my own venture was the beginning of my exploration.

"NO" IS A COMPLETE SENTENCE

After moving to another company I had a conversation with my manager about a position opening in another area at the time. I was working on a contract that was coming to an end and my manager was diligently trying to find a landing spot for her team. When I spoke to the hiring manager, I declined the offer for an interview. It may sound crazy, but I truly felt in my heart that it was not the move for me. Here's the whole truth, I believed that the next move I made was going to be out the door to my home office where I could devote more time to my business. Sounds crazy, right? When I had the discussion with my manager about the decline she was astonished at my "no." In fact, when I gave her my decision she flat out asked "Why?" Then followed that up with lots of other questions. That was an uncomfortable moment for me. I appreciated that she was doing what a good manager would do—look out for her employees—but I didn't feel I could tell her that the real reason I was declining her offer was because I was positioning myself to work for me! Nope, it wasn't time to share that information. It was one of those times when I had to stand behind my decision and not allow someone else's "why" to cause me to doubt myself.

I'd done that way too many times. Once upon a time I would have second-guessed my decision and beat myself up when someone confronted me. Not this time. This time I stood in my power. You might be thinking, "She was crazy for turning down that opportunity to at least have a conversation." All I can say is that sometimes you have a feeling about something that you just know is right, but you can't get others to understand. This was one of those times.

So, there are times when we must stay right where we are to get the lesson and new assignment. While many of my colleagues were excited about their years of service—I was too in the beginning of my career—it was becoming clearer that longevity in fulfilling someone else's dream wasn't so significant.

This feeling grew more intense. Still, I knew this wasn't something that I could share with everyone. I had a few close friends and family that I would talk to but, for the most part, I held it close. My heart and spirit were whispering, "There's something more for you and you need to begin to uncover and explore it fully." If there was a quote bubble above my head when I was having that conversation with my manager about the interview I declined, this would have been in big, bold letters!

CHAPTER 3

What Would You Do for Free

Ask yourself, 'what would I do for free?' Then go do that!
— Author Unknown

Have you ever thought about what you absolutely love doing? Many would confess that their 9 to 5 isn't really it. That job may keep the lights on, but it doesn't bring you joy. It's what we *have* to do, not necessarily what we *want* to do, which means we spend a good portion of our lives in a state of doing, not in a state of being. I was watching the first episode of *The Van Jones Show* on CNN where Van was interviewing Shawn "Jay-Z" Carter and Jay-Z talked about how we confuse having a job with our purpose. I remember hanging on to these words even when they moved on to a new conversation. There is so much truth to that! But here's the thing, because we don't always make that distinction we get caught in the act of doing.

Doing can look like you're just going through the motions. Same routine. Same people. Different day of the week. But being is about a deeper sense of satisfaction and fulfillment. There are certain things that just warm your heart. Consequently, you find yourself in a natural rhythm while doing them, sometimes without thought. You may be doing "it" for friends and family right now with little to no effort, without even realizing it. What is "it?' "It" is that thing that you'd stay up all night working on, then get up the next day and do it all over again. Or "it" may wake you up in the middle of the night because ideas are flowing through your mind like a river, and you just can't sleep.

This used to happen to me back in 2006 when I got the vision to start my own business. Until then, having my own business had never occurred to me. After all, I was the first on my mother's side of the family to graduate college. Soon after graduating from Frostburg State University, I married my college sweetheart and we did what most middle-class people do—we got an apartment. Two years later we bought our first house then had our first child. We were living the life that we were told to prepare for. With our two incomes we were doing okay.

SPIRITUAL AWAKENING

Then in 2006 something changed. I went to church for a Ladies Night Out Revival. Toward the end of the service the minister prepared to collect the offering. Her words still ring in my ear: "I'm asking for a donation of twenty dollars. For some of you it won't come back to you monetarily. It'll come back to you in an idea." I reached into my purse and realized that all I had was twenty dollars. "But," I thought, "I need gas. If I give these twenty dollars what will I do?" I kept listening to the minister's gentle plea. As I listened I felt a pull within me, guiding me to give that twenty. I reluctantly chose to be obedient. The very next day I was sitting at my desk at work, a quiet space back in the corner by a window—I loved that spot because it was so hidden. As I sat there a sea of ideas started rushing in. Suddenly I had a vision to open a day spa. The ideas were clear but confusing—clear in the sense that the thoughts were very vivid and succinct, yet confusing because I had never thought anything like that before. As the ideas flowed I started writing them down. These intense thoughts flowed for days. I found myself researching how to write a business plan and how I could pull all the pieces together. Wait! What was happening? This was not part of my plan.

Yet, the ideas kept coming; so much that I started keeping a pen and paper on my bathroom counter and nightstand. Things would pop into my head at night. I would get up, write them down then go back to bed. The next day I would add the scribbled notes to my journal, then try to make sense of them later. Or a thought would come during the course of the day that would rush in like a clear burst of light. It was so new and so overwhelming that I remember stopping to ask, "God, is this You or is this me being silly with wishful thinking?"

ASK AND YOU WILL BE ANSWERED

Fasting opens us up to revelation and confirmation. So I decided that I was going on a three day fast. I really hungered for the answer to the above question. Monday through Wednesday I drank nothing but water from early morning until late afternoon and prayed throughout the day. On Thursday, after the fast, I went to Bible Study. My Pastor walked back and forth as he taught the lesson.

He paused, as if he was taking a detour in the lesson to go another route. Then he said, "The Lord told some of you to start a business and you've been asking yourself, 'Is this you God?'" I stood there, tears flowing, feeling like God had spoken right to me through my Pastor.

That was one of the deepest spiritual encounters I'd had in my life. I saw a direct connection between me seeking answers, fasting and getting clarity. I got my answer, and it gave me the fuel to keep writing my business plan, still I was also nervous because I had no idea what I was about to embark on.

As I wrote the plan, I also started seeing a connection between what I visualized for the day spa and a new passion for well-being on all levels—mind, body and spirit. I found myself thinking about living well and what that looked like, how my spa would allow me to provide the services I wanted to deliver so that my clients would have a complete wellness experience. In the midst of all of this, I began noticing something else that I hadn't paid much attention to before. I seemed to be the ear that friends were looking for when they needed to talk. I became the listener when they were in crisis or just needed a sounding board. They came to me for comfort, encouragement, and laughter. Consequently, when I was asked I offered insight and support. This felt right to me. I loved when friends would come to my desk and sit in my "visitor's chair" to talk.

Sometimes it was work related, other times personal. These moments reminded me how much people need an outlet, a place of release and refuge. My kind ear, coupled with the day spa concept, felt like it was shaping up to be a good thing. I loved thinking about what I could do and events I could plan that would give people that outlet. It was natural and rewarding for me. So I could play around with my ideas around the spa I started organizing special events in my home for friends and family. I was able to share my joy of doing events and provide opportunities for people to relax and enjoy "me" time. I called it practice, for when the spa opened!

SPACE FOR RENEWAL

I hosted a girls' spa day for a neighbor and her girlfriends. She wanted an intimate gathering—but not in her house—so we agreed to do it in my home. I had it all together—the ambiance, the smell, the music, the food and the massage therapists. I even had a check-in form on my computer, so I could account for the ladies when they arrived. The women could not believe what they were experiencing. They repeatedly said how much they needed that release, how it felt like they were in a real spa. My soul stirred with joy!

I felt so much excitement planning the activities, menus and putting everything together. Every time I planned an event I was so full of energy. I was often the last person in the house to go to bed because I wanted to make sure everything was right. Then I'd be the first to rise, to finish anything left undone from the night before. When the event was over I'd get even more thrilled from the feedback from my guests. AND I WAS DOING IT FOR FREE! I wasn't getting paid in dollars to create the spa experience, but I was being rewarded knowing there was a satisfied patron, and I got to do what made my heart sing.

> Tap into it. Explore what makes your
> heart sing, because that's the gift
> you're meant to give the world.

My satisfaction came from knowing that I was able to create an amazing experience for them. Money can't buy that feeling. Nor can words sufficiently capture such sentiments. Each gathering inspired me to plan the next thing. I was in an exciting place. What's more, I knew these experiences were just the beginning of the journey.

Right now for you there's something that you do and it's costing you nothing but seamless, natural effort. It's the thing YOU would do for free because it's what you love to do. Whether you realize it or not, it's your gift, your purpose, your destiny. It's what you were put on this earth to do but maybe you've never thought of it as your purpose. Maybe you enjoy writing or sewing. Maybe you can dance or you're good with children. Perhaps you have a tender heart for the elderly. Maybe you're a good listener or speaker. Whatever "it" is it's a gift, like a beautifully wrapped box with a big bow that has your name on it. Think about it for a minute. What do people come to you for? What do they look to you to help them solve? When they seek your help, how does it make you feel? The answers to these questions are clues to that gift. And when you use your gift you're like a kid on Christmas morning opening the present, your gift, with excitement and anticipation!

UNWRAPPING YOUR GIFTS

There may be times when you prick your finger on a staple that holds the bow together, or get a paper cut from the wrapping paper. Yes, these are much like the bumps and bruises we experience in life. But you keep opening gifts because you want to see what's inside, right? It's this nervous kind of excitement about exploring what you love that allows you to operate on adrenaline. You just move in your natural flow of things. This is your seal, your mark, your stamp of purpose.

And let me add this, you may start off doing "it" for free, but in time discover a way to monetize your gifts. Know that that's perfectly okay. In fact, I believe The Creator intends for us to do just that, because then we better position ourselves to use our gifts to bless others in countless ways. You'll need to decide if, when, and how to transition from "free giving" to monetizing your message or service. But always leave yourself open to that possibility!

Now, you may have already discovered your purpose. If so, maybe it's time you take it to a new level or find new opportunities to expand on it. So what are you waiting for? Why not begin to unwrap the gifts that are on the inside of you? They're there, waiting for you to tap into them. So, go ahead. Act like it's Christmas morning and the kid in you is ready to have at it!

GIVE YOURSELF PERMISSION

If you're like so many others, despite your best intentions there are times when instead of moving forward you hesitate. You might figure, it's just a silly ole' hobby. It's just something I do on the side, something I have fun with.

You look at the box, the gift, and start to open it. But wait, there's this little nagging feeling that makes you question whether this new discovery is really worth investing energy into. You hesitate. "Well, other people are already doing this. I'll do it for free; it's so small. "How could it be my special gift, let alone my purpose?" your self-talk demands.

Well, think about it this way. Your gift is unique to you. It may be *similar* to what someone else does, but the *way* you do it, share it, deliver it is what makes it special. So don't get hung up on someone else's gift. Focus on you and what it is you can offer the world. And remember, seemingly insignificant things have value. For example, maybe you have a unique way of being organized. It might seem like a small thing. You might even fancy yourself as a bit obsessive/compulsive. Do you get that loads of people struggle with clutter and disorganization?

These people need you. Whatever you do, don't underestimate the value of your gift to help people create orderly, serene, lovely spaces in their homes and offices. Disorganized people are waiting on you to make yourself available. Don't deny them.

So, what would *you* do for free? Follow these steps to figure that out:

1. Get yourself a journal that's small enough to carry with you every day. Phones, tablets and iPads are great, but writing with pen and paper is a powerful

tool and an age-old habit that brings ideas to life by getting them out of your head and on paper.

2. As different things come to you during the course of the day, write them down. Tune in to things you do and conversations you have with people that make you feel good, that bring a smile to your face and gives you a sense of peace. Notice what you daydream about and write it down, even if it seems to make no sense or be connected.

   For example, you might notice that conversing with a neighbor who lives alone is easy, and that you feel good when you help them with groceries and chores. Write your observations down. This may lead you to provide a concierge service for people who don't like to grocery shop!

3. As you write things down, get in the habit of looking at what you've written. This will help you identify patterns of behavior that will call your gifts to the forefront and help you become more present to them as you use them. This will be key as you continue on this journey, the journey that will give you the freedom to be you, someone operating in life on purpose!

CHAPTER 4

Eyesight vs. Vision

"Vision is the art of seeing what is invisible to others."
– Jonathan Swift

I n 2013, I became an active member of a network marketing company. Many people have their opinions about network marketing, and debate whether you can really achieve success in them. For me it worked very well and here's the reason why. It was my first time being connected to something outside of my church, that helped me expand my thinking. In fact, it was an enhancement to the faith principles that guide me.

I remember one night our regional group was hosting a team call and I was asked to share something that would motivate us for the week. I had been hearing a lot from the leaders in the company about having vision and how we often limit ourselves because we can't imagine a successful outcome. I was like this in my early adult years and I'd witnessed this same myopia in those in my own circles.

Some of the people I knew would have to first see something in black and white before they would believe or buy into it. As I got older and met people outside of my familiar environments, it became apparent to me that there was a huge difference between eyesight and vision. On that night when it was my turn to share a motivational message with our team, I felt a passion about this topic that I'd never expressed before. Perhaps it was because I never understood how polar opposite the two words were and how much of a role they play in how we see ourselves in the world.

Understand that identifying the thing you would do for free is the fun part of the journey. The fact that it's something you enjoy, makes you laugh, or feels good and are passionate about means its easily recognizable. Once you begin to see it, it shows up for you over and over again. What you may not realize is where that excitement can take you, mainly because it's sometimes hard to identify when you're operating in your day-to-day world where everything is familiar. This is where eyesight versus vision comes into play, and though they may appear to be the same thing, the two are very different.

CHECK YOUR LENS

Eyesight is the physical ability to see the things around you, whether it's the trees, flowers, a painting, or the face of a loved one. Eyesight keeps you present to your reality and what's going on in your space. With eyesight you can see what is in your bank account or your closet. You can gaze at the sky. Vision, on the other hand, is not a physical faculty at all. Vision is the image that we hold in our mind of that which we long for. Having vision isn't dependent on where we come from, what we've been through or what we have. It's not tangible or visible to the natural eye. With vision you can see the future. You can see what you DESIRE to have in your bank account, your closet, your relationships. Because with vision you have the power to dream of what could be. Vision inspires you to put faith into action as it empowers you to step into the realm of pure possibility.

> Dare to expand your creativity
> beyond what your eyes can see.

You're here, at a decision point. Here is where you can begin to create a vision for the thing you would do for free. Or, you can let your eyesight show you all the ways that you can't. In order to put your vision to the test, to allow you to transition from doing what you love to making it the purpose for which you serve is going to require something. It will require you to knock down the cobwebs, unlock the dungeon door and move the vision to the forefront of your mind. Remember, though, that eyesight will tell you that there is absolutely no way the vision can come to pass, that you don't have the money, the time, the resources, or the energy. You're not skilled enough. Nobody has ever done that before. There's no way you can do it. So many people are doing it already; it doesn't make sense for you to do it, too. These are the voices of eyesight; it relies solely on what is seen in the natural. When you consider the thing you would do for free and you start to think of how you can turn that excitement and passion about it into your purpose, your eyesight will try to hold the vision hostage. You're the one, my friend, who holds the key. Now is the time to decide whether you'll just stand there with the keys in your hand or unlock the dungeon gate and walk out of the prison of your limited mind.

RATTLE THE CAGE

If you're still reading that means you've decided to unlock the gate, or at least rattle the cage! And don't mistake this escape as your freedom ticket because you will have to constantly conquer the battle of eyesight versus vision, i.e., what you believe can and cannot happen. There will be moments that challenge you, especially when you decide to really take action toward doing what you love.

See, finding and living in your purpose is not just about figuring out what you would do for free and then moving toward it in a way that allows you to live fulfilled, but it's about recognizing that in order to do that there are some things that need to happen first. Yes, our vision must inspire the belief that "this is possible," but the vision alone won't get you there. You're but in the beginning phase of the process, where you sometimes gain traction and spin your wheels, simultaneously. You're moving but not sure how you're going to get there.

I know. I've been there. How do you think this book came to be? I will admit that when I was sitting under that hair dryer in my room in 2007 outlining this book, I saw it through the lens of my eyesight. I knew the purpose. I knew some of the content. But I lacked the vision of how to bring it forth. Years later, more life experiences and personal growth gave me a sharper view of my purpose and a different perspective of what I'd share in this book.

Listen, this is where you decide that you're going to take action. Want to know why? Sure you do. Well, there comes a time when you desire something more. Once you recognize your gifts and passions, and you begin to have a vision for what you really want you're now uncomfortable. Some days you'll feel like you're just going through the motions, plagued by the feeling that there's got to be something more. Your spirit starts to call you to it, even if you don't know what "it" is yet. What might this look like? You get up in the morning excited about the new day, get dressed, drive to work, and then punch the clock. But you're awash with excitement about checkout time.

Yes, you feel the discontent. Don't get me wrong; I'm sure you're grateful for your 9 to 5 because it keeps the lights on, food on the table and a roof over your head. The reality is that you're constantly learning something on your 9 to 5 that you could use whether you stay in that job or leave. But when purpose comes a knocking, that gnawing feeling of discontent won't stop until you answer the door.

CHAPTER 5

Planning and Patience

*I know God has a plan. I pray for direction to follow it,
patience to wait on it, and knowledge to know when it comes.*
— *Author Unknown*

I used to coordinate weddings, family events and vacations. So I am very good at planning things—maybe even too meticulous at times! When I was planning my wedding, I'd meet with my bridesmaids and hostesses armed with a typed agenda and specific instructions. My mom and sister would probably tell you how much I got on their nerves with all the details and wanting things done a certain way. You might be wondering what could be wrong with a bride-to-be making sure everything was accounted for. Not a thing. Except I was a royal pain in the ass! I was very inpatient, pouting and unwilling to budge from my plans. My husband would always say, "It's either your way or no way!" This was my attitude toward just about everything.

Then I started getting some in-your-face lessons that were the catalysts for my becoming less rigid. I share quite of few of them in this book.

Once you have identified what you love to do, or at least have thought about how you can take your passion to a new level, the next step is planning your purpose. When you identify the thing that resonates with you, the thing you would do for free (but would be grateful to get paid for), you are ready to plot a course of action, one that gets you closer to where you want to be or takes you to that next level if you're already using your gift. The journal that you started using in chapter 2 now becomes the blueprint for you to do that; it's where your purpose takes shape, where you discover new possibilities, how to create (or recreate) yourself and decide how you will play in the world. It's the place where you take notes, set your goals, write your affirmations, make your lists and stay connected with yourself. It's where the thing you would do for free gives birth to ways to monetize that gift, if this is your desire.

> At some point you have to step
> beyond your comfort zone, stop
> over-analyzing and take action.

So often we fail to plan. We make excuses. Things get in the way. We're like the child on Christmas who'd much rather play with the box than the toy in the box.

We don't think it's possible, so we don't even bother to yearn, dream, plan, and expect the gift to transform into something that could bring unspeakable joy and contentment for ourselves and others. Even worse, when and if we do develop the plan, we fail to work it! We write. We think. We over think. We rethink. We seek counsel. We pray and then...we wait. Before you know it, nothing happens. Time passes. We return to our "old normal," another dream deferred. What's our old normal? You know, those are the conditions and circumstances that everyone is engaging in on a daily basis and complaining about. They're the conditions that we grew up with, that were instilled in us from our families, schools and communities.

Stuff like, "We can't afford it, so don't even think about it!" and, "Do well in school so you can get a good job." Or, "These skills will take you a long way with a good company." I'm not suggesting that these statements don't have some merit, or that they couldn't serve you on some level; but living on purpose, planning and moving to action will require a *new* normal. OK, maybe in your youth your family really didn't have money for certain things, something I know quite well. But at some point, we've got to cut the psychological and emotional umbilical cords that tie us to our old normal so we are free to create something new for ourselves. Creating a new normal is also about taking skills and experiences gleaned from school and those good jobs and utilizing them in new ways.

IGNITE YOUR PASSION

Planning your purpose and moving into action is also birthed from something more deeply rooted than just excitement about your gifts. These things come from DESIRE!

DESIRE is what **D**rives **E**very **S**tep **I**n **R**eaching your **E**xcellence. This means you have a reason, or a "why" that pushes you into making a plan and taking the action to execute it.

33

Everything you do is with your "why" in mind. You could have a passion for helping people, creating a legacy for your family, eliminating money as the reason for why you can't do something, building a new level of confidence within yourself, changing your diet or losing weight, or all of the above. DESIRE will move fear, doubt, excuses and procrastination out of the way. Or give you a plan for working around them. It'll make you find a way to turn your gifts into something that'll make you leap out of bed in the mornings filled with passion and gratitude for life. By the way, DESIRE isn't just about getting you to plan your purpose and move into action, but DESIRE is something to hold onto on the journey. In fact, you may have to grip DESIRE tighter and tighter as you move forward because there will come a time when you'll feel like quitting.

Trust me. That time WILL come. And if you've let go of your DESIRE you WILL quit, only to leave your gift in the box and your purpose unfulfilled. This is especially true when you begin to plan, and things don't look like what you expect. Here is another place where desire plus its partner, flexibility, is essential.

Understand that when the plan changes and you're led to go right when you set out for left nothing's wrong. And don't question your gift or purpose. In fact, consider that the alleged detour could put you on a path where one, or all, of these things can happen:

- You discover new things about yourself.
- You meet new people who are directly connected to the work you will do while operating in your purpose.

- You meet people you are meant to serve as part of your purpose.

Either way, desire and flexibility must be committed partners. I had to face this reality when I discovered I would design events and share information with people about living well mentally, physically and spiritually well for free. When I wrote my business plan back in 2006 for the big dream, I knew that my purpose was to provide outlets for people to take care of themselves. Initially my plan was to use things like massages, facials, fitness and meditation in a spa environment. I was looking at building spaces, and even had a floor plan drawn up, which is still on my vision board to this day.

It was a huge and costly endeavor, and at the time a tremendous risk for my family even though I knew that's what business-minded people did, they took risks. I did all the legwork of writing the business plan, had my accountant review the details, paraded the plan in front of a bank executive who said, "It's one of the best business plans that I've seen in a long time." I sought investors, even though I wasn't really sure how to navigate all the details. I was inexperienced, excited and nervous all at once.

Surprise! Surprise! Then there was a pregnant pause.

Then I got pregnant. I was completely surprised because it was so unexpected. My daughter was nine years old. My husband and I had been trying for years to have another child; so for it to happen at this point in time, nine years later, was truly mind-blowing. I believed, however, that things were in divine order. When my cute baby boy was born and I was home on maternity leave, not only did I enjoy this new blessing but it made me stop and re-evaluate my plan. I felt strongly about what

DELAY NOT DENIAL

I was passionate about, so I had to figure out how I could make something work without taking out a large business loan. I also had to understand the message behind the pause.

Now I had a newborn to tend to and provide for. Oh, and did I mention we had a new house? All of these factored into the equation. So, even though I started the plan and moved into action feeling like I was coasting toward my vision, I soon realized I had to revamp how my purpose was to be executed. I still had the same passion and excitement about helping people to live well, but I was unsure about *how* I was going to make it all happen. Things were looking very different from what I saw in my mind. I had to put my original plan on hold, and this made me wonder if I'd indeed received the right vision.

You know how it is when things don't go our way, the disappointment and frustration can leave us wading through the "what happened?" blues. This is a human response to sudden detours. We very often start our journey with our final destination in view. Then we get pushed to the right and pulled to the left...when we imagined it was going to be a straight and predicable path. Other times we may be forced to stop, when we think we should be moving full steam ahead. That was me. I was ready to execute the business plan because of all the hard work I had poured into it; so it was a hard pill to swallow when the Creator stuck a bookmark in the middle of my story. Looking back on things, I now know His infinite wisdom was so much greater than mine. I was planning when the stock market was volatile—people were losing businesses and homes. The economy was in a bad way, and if everything had aligned as I'd planned there's a high probability that I would have suffered extreme financial strain, like so many others were during that time. I realize now that that wasn't the right time for this part of the vision to unfold.

This was probably one of the hardest areas for me because, in my mind, I was ready to put myself to the challenge. After all, I had done my research and had all the key components to my plan—my mission, vision, financials, charts, statistics, and competitors' information. I WAS READY!

Actually, I really wasn't ready for what I'd planned. Though I didn't quite understand it then, I accepted this as fact, so after careful thought and prayer I was led to change the plan.

NEW REVELATIONS

One afternoon I was standing in my kitchen when suddenly an idea hit me over the head like a ton of bricks. Instead of the brick and mortar wellness spa, I would act as a broker of spa services! I would partner with clients and licensed professionals to deliver services potential clients were looking for. WOW! This was the revelation that inspired me to start hosting spa parties in my home.

There was something very calming and reassuring about this new idea. I felt like I was on to something that would allow me to keep moving forward with less risk. This eliminated the overhead costs of maintaining a building and the need to hire, train and pay employees. So the delay was a blessing. Here I was with this brand new approach to fulfilling my dream. And guess what, it brought with it an unimaginable calm and peace. I'm not telling you there weren't moments of doubt and fear and confusion.

I absolutely experienced angst and anxiety from time to time. But it was a beautiful blessing. Even with the change in direction, I was still able to cater to my clients and plan events for them as if they were in a day spa. There was no need to kick and scream, rant and rage because my plan didn't come to be as I intended. I felt in my heart that everything happened for a reason. As it turns out, the delay was exactly what was needed for that time. What I didn't realize then was that I still had some growing pains ahead. This was still the beginning of the journey, so I tucked the business plan away in a temporary holding place, shifted the direction of my sail, and kept moving in the wind.

PURPOSE PRINCIPLES

- When we get clear about what we would do for free it is imperative to create a plan. Remember the adage, "If you fail to plan, you plan to fail." However, in planning don't get stuck in the pie in the sky or the all or nothing mentality. That is, don't fall for the lie that you have to accomplish the whole dream, or fulfill your entire life's purpose, in one fell swoop.

The day spa was it for me because it was bigger than anything I had ever conceived of for myself, but I realized that taking baby steps were great and surprisingly rewarding. You will discover that over time your passion will take you to different levels of your purpose, and as that happens you will need to re-plan so you'll be prepared to approach each level with new strategies and goals. You may even see extensions of your purpose manifesting in different ways, as I did.

- Secondly, as you embrace the beauty of taking baby steps, remember to be FLEXIBLE. You'll need flexibility to adapt and adjust to new insights and alternate routes. Even if things don't unfold as you originally mapped them out, it's okay. You should still be able to identify the underlying theme of your purpose in that plan. At one time I was so rigid in my thinking, and I believe this was as much about stripping some of that away as it was about bringing more clarity to my purpose.

- I'll be honest, I wanted to open that day spa when I first started writing my business plan, and when that didn't happen according to my plan I wondered whether I misinterpreted what I believed was divine direction. Then that delay eventually led me to discovering new gifts that I was unaware of. The gifts were still related to wellness, but if you had asked me then if I would have written this book and spearheaded my other projects I would have said "NO WAY!" Ultimately, everything was divinely orchestrated. Trust in that for you too!

CHAPTER 6

Past Tense

Your past is the Place that Anchors a Strong Testimony.
– Ericka Sallee

H ave you ever picked up a new book, flipped through it, then headed for the end of the story to see what happened? Or perhaps you've scanned the pages of a magazine before looking at the table of contents because an article or picture caught your eye. But if we're looking for something in the magazine that we can't find we have to go back to the table of contents to direct us to the right page, right? Well, that's the same way we treat our dreams. When we discover the thing we're willing to do for free then come up with a plan of attack we've essentially jumped to the middle of the book. This is okay, because we need something to fire us up that'll give us a needed dose of adrenaline so we can keep pressing toward making our "it" happen.

However, you must understand this: *you still have to go back and start from the beginning of the book, especially if you intend to finish it.* What does this mean? It means you have to go back to *your* beginning to revisit the stuff that will make you appreciate the plot of *your* story.

This is where I found myself. I was thrilled about the things that were unfolding in my life, but I also knew there were rather heavy matters in my past that I needed to address. Let's face it; all of us have them. Many are things that we're not proud of, and we think that because of them we can't possibly have a fulfilling future, certainly not one where we get to be a blessing to others. The truth is, these are growing pains we must navigate through.

HEARTFELT MEMORIES

I think back to my childhood. I come from a loving family so I have very fond memories of my childhood. Family celebrations for holidays, birthdays or just because were so special. These were held at my aunt's, what we affectionately called "The House" because that's where all the family events took place. There was always plenty of good food, laughter and fun. I was the baby in the family for a long time so I always got lots of attention. My mom, grandmother, aunts, uncles and cousins spoiled me. I can remember playing Hopscotch and Dodge Ball and running around outside until the street lights came on; I was so carefree. I didn't go to summer camp but summertime was just so cool and laid back. Corn on the cob, watermelon and cucumber salad with mayonnaise (not salad dressing) and salt and pepper were standards on hot days. My kids enjoy these to this day! At Christmas time our living room was like a toy store with endless boxes wrapped in beautiful paper and toys galore. My grandmother loved putting angel hair on the Christmas tree but I hated it because it made me itch like crazy. Nonetheless, that is still a pleasant memory.

I was the only child for ten years. When my sister came along I thought I had my very own doll baby, and she had a second mother. Although now she'll tell you how much that annoyed her as we got older! My sister was so fat and cuddly, with cute little dimples. These are the memories that bring me pure joy. In my early teens I spent summers at my cousin Ronnie's house. I never wanted to go home. We had our share of fun...and mischief!

PAIN POINTS

> Our pain points are like plant
> fertilizer, it helps us grow.

But amid the cherished times of my childhood were also moments that weren't so fun. My mom, a single mother, struggled to raise me on her own. We never went without the basics and family support was strong. But times were hard. I remember having to go to the store with food stamps. At that time, there was no EBT card that could pass as a debit card. It was paper "money" that was clearly not real money. Everybody could see you were on public assistance. That was embarrassing, and I cringed at the thought of being in line in front of someone from school.

I didn't have some of the stuff other kids had, like the name brand shoes and clothes. And, though my clothes were clean and decent, none of that mattered to kids who delighted in teasing and ridiculing me. Trying to fit in and be part of the in-crowd was difficult because they liked who they liked and wouldn't bother with those they didn't like.

Instead, they enjoyed taunting, teasing and humiliating us outsiders.

I remember dressing for school one morning, trying on an outfit that I was unsure of. So I asked a neighbor if it looked okay, since my mom had already left for work. I had on jeans, long leg warmers that came up over my knees, and some cowboy boots that were given to me. Today that outfit would be very much en vogue, but back then I had my doubts. I just didn't feel completely comfortable in it. I'll never forget what my neighbor said, "Oh Ericka, you know it looks fine!" No, I didn't know that. It was different. I was trying to create something new, trying to make my own fashion statement. So Miss Vera's words gave me a confidence boost. I was feeling good and ready to take that middle school stroll through the halls with my friend first thing that morning. You know, that's what we did back then when we thought we looked good. So me and my friend started walking. We got about half way down the hallway when I felt their eyes on me and heard people laughing. That's when I knew my fashion statement was a fashion bust. My heart sank. I felt so stupid and ashamed.

CONFIDENCE AND SELF-ESTEEM

The irony was that I was also teased and threatened for thinking I was cute. It didn't make sense to me. On the one hand I was laughed at and made to feel inferior. On the flip side I was the target of envy and jealousy.

Confusing, right? Tell me about it! I'll never forget the time when a girl followed me home from school, taunting me the whole way. Of course the spectators followed us, exacerbating the situation, which made me even more nervous and scared. When we got to my apartment building, in front of my door, she pushed me and it was on. I fought back, but since that was my first fight ever I wasn't sure I knew what to do. What I did know was this: I wasn't about to stand there and get the beat down and not put up a good fight! I was scared but I had to protect myself. Finally a maintenance worker broke it up and the girl went on her way. I called my mother at work to tell her what happened. She was livid that she was not there to protect me. I was boohooing. I was so upset that I cursed. Well, my mother checked me VERY QUICKLY, so I didn't do *that* again! Even though I was traumatized, I insisted that I got the best of that girl! I can still see it like it was yesterday. I'd pinned her up against the door as I wondered to myself, "What in the world will happen next?" I can tell you this, that girl never bothered me again.

Why don't they just leave me alone?

Another time some girls followed me home, wanting to fight. When I ran in the house and told my mom, who was seven months pregnant with my sister Toshah at the time, she had the nerve to come outside and yell, "If y'all wanna fight, come over here and fight her now!" I was thinking to myself, "Is she crazy?" Needless to say, they quickly backed down. When they saw mom they immediately shrank from big, bad wolves to ants. Boy, was I relieved. Like the other girl, they never bothered me again.

Even still, I kept trying to figure out what it was that made people so mean to me. I never bothered or provoked anyone. Nor was I a troublemaker. I guess that was the nature of the awkward adolescent years. Everything was at play—menstrual cycle, hormones, cute boys, cruel girls, trying to fit in, wanting to be liked. So all of this, plus trying to avoid getting beat up, was tough. I even think back to elementary school, when a girl made faces at me the entire class and threatened me with, you guessed it, a fight! Her menacing glare, and the promise of getting banged in the face made fear rise up in me so much that all I could do was sit there as my legs shook uncontrollably. I don't quite recall how the situation was diffused. Maybe the teacher saw me and addressed it. That part I can't remember. I just know we never fought. To this day though I can vividly remember how terrified and helpless I felt not knowing how I was going to protect myself and prevail.

IMAGE IS MORE THAN A REFLECTION

As I look back now, I realize these were the moments directly tied to my own insecurities and struggles with confidence and self-esteem.

I felt powerless in most of those situations. It never occurred to me that there was something in me that intimidated and threatened other people. I'm not bragging or boasting, nor am I, as they say, conceited. I'm sure you can relate. I'd bet there have been moments in your life just like those, where you have been afraid, or even worse, maybe you have projected fear on to someone else. Think about it, what better way to feel big than to make other people feel small and powerless? Walking in your purpose requires that you too recognize your power. But when you face situations where you feel stripped of your power, seldom do you realize how much of it we have.

So, for quite some time I didn't realize I had this inner strength. I knew I had enemies, who, seemingly, were more in control of me than I was of myself. But I never suspected that *I* had power. Such was the case for me as an 11-year-old girl. This time it wasn't the girls who chased me down and provoked fights. They were just being mean and doing what girls have always done, be catty. This was something altogether different. This was about a grown man who decided to exercise power over me and my innocence. I don't even know if he's still alive. Honestly, I don't recall seeing him since the incident, which happened more than thirty years ago. Our neighbors were cordial. They'd speak to us; we'd speak to them.

We were friendly like most residents in an apartment building where everybody knew everybody. I spent a lot of time at their house after school watching MTV. This was back when you could time what videos were coming on because they had the same schedule every day.

> Sometimes the people closest to us
> are the ones that hurt us the most.

One evening I was at my neighbor's house and the enemy was standing in the kitchen in front of the sink. I went in happily, like I had done many times before. There was small talk. Another relative was there too. She was usually there at the house cooking, cleaning and washing while the other adults were away during the day. As I stood there talking I noticed that the relative was standing near the entrance, between the kitchen and the living room. It was odd, but I didn't think much of it then. It was then that the enemy grabbed me and kissed me deep and hard in the mouth, like a man kisses a grown woman not a child. I was so shocked, and I wasn't sure what to do. I just remember feeling awkward, frightened and excited. Why was it exciting and how in the world could I say that? Well, therein lies the confusing part. There was something inside of me that knew full well that this was terribly wrong while another part of me wondered if this was what it felt like to be wanted and accepted. I had struggled so much with wanting to be liked, wanting to fit in and fighting my way through, so this "affection" was something new, different and exciting. It was magical, confusing, and wrong all at once.

When the enemy released me I stepped back awash with embarrassment. I could no longer look him in the face, so I ran out of the kitchen and pass the person I thought was a friend. As it turns out, she was the lookout because the enemy's wife was in the bedroom with the door shut. I went home with this strange, dirty little secret. I ran straight to my room and cried. I never mentioned a word to my mother about it until many years later.

SLAY THE DRAGON

What had I done to cause this to happen and how could I explain it? Was it going to happen again? Who would believe me, and would the enemy's wife be mad at me? As I sat in my room, I decided to bury what happened. As the tears silently rolled down my cheeks they formed a dam of silence. In the days that followed I steered clear of that house and the enemy. I don't even remember seeing them much after that. Things were different, yet I pretended everything was the same by remaining silent to what would forever be seared in the recesses of my mind. It escapes me who moved away first, but when we finally did leave I carried more with me than just the things that we packed in boxes. I now know that what happened was not my fault and recognize that the incident was less about what was taken from me and more about what I gained: *I gained the courage to talk about it and perhaps help someone else deal with the dragons in their closet.*

I was driving home from work one day, listening to the news on the radio about the #metoo movement. Story after story was about women in Hollywood, corporate America and "next door" who had experienced sexual assault or sexual harassment at the hands of powerful men. They were speaking out and letting their voices be heard. As I listened, it hit me: I wasn't just *listening* to stories, I *am* a story. WOW! I picked up the phone and called my mom to share that realization with her. I had been listening to all these stories as if I was an outsider, like I couldn't relate. When actually, I knew full well what those women were going through. I had been there. Even though at this point in my life I had already shared my story with my mom about what happened to me as a young girl, I needed to share this aha! moment with her. Her gentle spirit and listening ear were a comfort to me. Instead of feeling embarrassed or ashamed I felt liberated. I was part of a club that I wish had no members, but I know change is needed and I believe it's coming.

FINDING FREEDOM

I won't mention names because I don't feel that it's relevant. What's significant about this part of my life is that I am honoring my need to be free. I had never told anyone about that incident, but I realized how much I needed to break my silence about this secret. That kitchen incident was one of the dragons in my closet that, while I wrestled with other issues in my life, needed to be slayed. As I shared what happened during therapy I experienced a sense of relief and peace. As a grown woman it's not so difficult to talk about.

Perhaps that's because I had nothing to prove to anyone, and I was no longer embarrassed. But there's a part of me that wonders how many other girls he did this to. I've also thought about what might have happened had I shared it earlier, when the incident happened. Many lives and relationships would have been impacted. I know I wasn't processing that then. I was just a confused young girl. But when I grew up I knew it was time to tell.

Like the time I was in college and in a relationship with this guy. It was nothing emotional, only physical. In fact, I should have stayed far, far, FAR away from him. But boy was he charming and charismatic.

Oh, and did I mention popular? All the girls wanted him. I guess you could say he was a "bad boy." I got caught in his web of compliments and sweet talk, the kind that makes you think you're special and the only one, which, as you undoubtedly guessed, couldn't have been further from the truth.

One day we were hanging out in my dorm room with friends, just chillin'. We were shooting the breeze and laughing about silly stuff. It happened seamlessly. One minute he was playfully tapping me on my shoulder and back, like boys tease girls they like. The next minute he was dragging me across the floor. At first it was funny, like it was just part of our silly banter. Then it got really rough, and I got scared. Our friends stopped laughing. I guess they too felt his behavior bordered on abusive. I tried to escape his grip but couldn't, and, as far as I could tell, he was getting a kick out of seeing me struggle to get away from him. One of my friends snapped, "Man, that's enough!" He just ignored him. I'm not sure what actually made him stop but eventually he let go of me and left the room. I got up off the floor feeling foolish and ashamed.

My friends and I looked at each other, trying to figure out what just happened. It was such a quick personality change that caught us all off guard, especially me! I should have jumped up and cursed at him to show him that I was not cool with what happened, even if he thought we were just playing around. I should have established a boundary, one that said I wasn't to be played with that way. But, well, I didn't. I was, however, meek and not in control. When I think about it now, I realize that though I physically got up, psychologically I was still on that floor—where I left my power. I didn't realize it then but that's exactly what I did. Someone violated me, and instead of standing up to him I allowed it to happen. Then I stood there speechless while another enemy walked out the door, leaving me confused and bewildered.

SET THE TONE

In the days that followed I didn't talk much about it because I was ashamed that it happened, and people had witnessed it. However, my relationship with this person changed. I never anticipated it lasting anyway, but that day caused a seismic shift. The reality is that I was a conquest. He moved on to conquer others before I could declare that I would have nothing else to do with him. That would have required me to be bold, but instead I allowed him to have the last say, so to speak.

My family and I were leaving the movies one evening. As we walked to the car we noticed that a group of teenagers were playing on the parking lot. A girl and a boy were horse playing around. I recall that he was being rather rough with her. She was laughing and giggling like it was cute.

Then I heard her scream, "Oh my God, he just banged me in my chest, like five times!" She continued to laugh as they ran off, out of sight. I felt this sickening feeling in my stomach that took me back to that day in my dorm when fun turned painful. I didn't stand up for myself and, in a sense, that's when I made it okay for people to mistreat me. This young girl was doing the exact same thing. She was setting the precedent for how she would allow herself to be treated by boys and men, and that made me sad and angry. I can't help but think about her, who she is, who she will become and how her relationships with men, and perhaps others, will be as a result of that incident. Though I could not reach that young woman that night, my hope is that you will understand the importance of knowing your worth and that you will teach girls and women in your life how to respect themselves so much that they will not tolerate disrespect and abuse from anyone.

HIDE AND SEEK

It's amazing how easy it is to give someone your power. Sometimes it happens so fast that you don't even realize how quickly you've given it up.

My experiences in school, my neighbor, my relationships were all times when I handed over my power. Tolerating the bullying, not telling my mom about what happened with my neighbor and letting guys disrespect and abuse me were all ways that I allowed myself to be stripped of dignity. Instead, I was hiding, wanting to break free from the past but not sure how.

The past is that thing that hides. Occasionally it sneaks around the corner of our minds just to see what we're up to. Some things don't rear their ugly head until we are well into our adulthood. We then find ourselves scratching our heads, trying to understand where our actions and behaviors come from. And why we keep doing the same old things expecting different results.

This is where we are challenged, where we get stuck because it's difficult to move forward on purpose until we deal with the painful past. The past peeks at us to see what we're going to do. Are we going to get a glimpse of it, get spooked and run and hide? Or are we going to face it? Sure, hiding may feel safe. But hiding means we not only miss the opportunity to conquer our past but then we're not available to be used to help others face shame, ridicule, embarrassment and hurt that threatens to rob them of their possibilities.

Nightmares about the past don't
have to destroy your dreams
of an amazing future.

IT'S OVER

So, what does our past say about us? Well, here's what I believe it says: we're like everybody else, we are flawed. We have bumps and bruises, scrapes and scars just like the next person. Don't get it twisted, EVERYBODY HAS SOMETHING. So, don't let anyone fool you into thinking your stuff is unique and therefore worse than theirs. Sure, it may be *different,* but so what? Ask yourself this question: *Did I ever say or do something to hurt myself or someone else?* If the answer is "yes," and I'm sure it is, then you have a past. Congratulations! But here is the breaking news—EVEN THOUGH YOU HAVE EXPERIENCED MOMENTS OF FAILURE, **YOU** ARE NOT A FAILURE! OK, it happened. Yes, it occurred. See that "ed" on the end of the word "happened," that means it is PAST TENSE. And once something happened that means it does not physically exist in the here and now, nor is it in your future…unless you put it there. So, leave it in the past where it rightfully belongs.

FORGIVE AND MOVE ON

I'm talking about the moments that keep us stuck in a place of despair, stuff that keeps us from walking in our purpose. There we are, stuck in our misery unable to see ourselves as the miracle that we are. We can't see we're someone who can touch and transform lives. We forget that we can recreate ourselves moment to moment. With one declaration we can change our present *and* create a beautiful future when we decide to leave the past right where it belongs, behind us! Haven't you heard: you can't drive forward while looking in the rearview mirror. It's impossible to move forward with our focus in the past. There will be naysayers and skeptics who will call us out, tell us that we'll never change, that there's no way we can recover from this or that, that they don't expect much from us. And they'll be downright cruel, whether they intend to be or not. Here's how to deal with that. Tell them to go look in the mirror and own where they are. Then you look in the mirror, forgive yourself and declare who you are! Don't keep a running tab on the past.

You know when you're out to eat, and not quite ready to close out your check so you keep it open and you keep ordering, adding to the bill? Then you finally ask for the check because you're now satisfied. It's the same way with the past. We revisit it, we talk about it, we get emotional about it, i.e., we keep that tab open, giving it energy and life when it really has served its purpose. Now it's time we let the past die.

OK, go ahead and acknowledge your past because that is part of the healing journey. And yet, this can take years for some people, just as it did with me. I didn't talk about the incident with my neighbor for 30 years! I encourage you to get professional help, if you need it, no matter what the stigma might be; that's a wise and healthy thing to do.

THERAPY IS HEALING

I did, and to be honest, it felt like a breath of fresh air to talk to someone who had no judgment. It was in therapy that I also talked about my relationship with my dad. I love my dad dearly, but we didn't have much of a relationship until I was fifteen. Prior to that, I never thought twice about having a dad because just about everyone I knew, with the exception of a few school friends, lived with their mom. Girls growing up without their dads was pretty much the norm in my circle. But one day I asked my mom about my dad, and through a series of events we began the journey of connecting me with him. This was how I ushered in my teen years. My parents were young when my mom got pregnant with me. Yes, I missed the early years of father-daughter bonding that naturally occurs when a father is lovingly involved in his daughter's life. I believe my relationship with boys and men may have been influenced by my father's absence. It's something that a girl learns from a dad's guidance. There is no blame. It's just part of my story. When I finally met my dad, something special happened though. We clicked instantly. I was nervous at the thought of meeting him for the first time. But when I laid eyes on him, I felt at ease and excited about the new chapter that was unfolding for the both of us. He was tall and handsome. It was as if all the missing years just slipped away. I can't really explain it because I've heard and read enough stories about similar situations that had a different outcome. I remember having a conversation with a family member who asked, "Aren't you angry or mad about the whole situation?" "No," I responded. Sure, there were questions. But anger?

Nope. And to be honest, the questions were minor. Why ask anyway? I didn't really care to bring up fifteen years' worth of the past because I was more excited about creating something new for the next fifteen years and beyond. I was young, so I felt joy at the thought of seeing and getting to know someone that I could now call daddy.

REFLECT AND RELEASE

Then of course, there are countless other mistakes from my high school, college and my adulthood years that play a major part in my history. Some of it is ugly, and I've gone through my range of emotions when I sit back and reflect on it all. I cannot, however, dwell there in the place of reflection. Reflections are good and necessary, but if we hang on to the memories too long they can create shadows. And shadows can get in the way of the sun. When we give life and energy to the mistakes, missteps, hurtful conversations, failures we're not free to move toward and walk confidently in our purpose. Acknowledgement and shifting ourselves in the right direction are necessary but constantly thinking about what we did wrong and weighing ourselves down with the negativity that stems from regret, shame and blame are counterproductive.

Remember, it's all a part of our purpose, whether it feels good or not. We can either let our past hinder us, or we can heal from it and allow it to help someone else. I chose healing. Which will you choose?

PURPOSE PRINCIPLES

- Remember that the past is a place where you learn and launch. This means you have teachable moments with yourself, to reflect on what happened, your role and what you would do differently given the same set of circumstances. Learn by getting in touch with the new you, the person who is capable of making good decisions, capable of living in integrity. Learning may even involve seeking professional help or hiring a coach who can help you get to the roots of the tree of your past. Investing time and money into professional services can help you find the support you need to be free of guilt, shame, embarrassment, pain, and humiliation. I've done it and I'm grateful for it.

- Then launch yourself into a new mindset, creating empowering ways of thinking about yourself and being in the world.

- **My P.A.S.T. is the <u>P</u>lace that <u>A</u>nchors <u>S</u>trong <u>T</u>estimony.** This means our past is the foundation that allows us to share how we've overcome and positions us to help someone else. Repeat the above bolded statement constantly throughout your day, until it vibrates in your spirit. In time this will become your truth.

- Accept the past as the past and not as a scarlet letter on your forehead.

- When someone tries to throw your past at you, DUCK! Maybe it sounds silly but get out of the way of negative words and attitudes. Shut down negative energy either by telling people you've moved on or end the relationship. Affirm yourself by constantly saying, *"The PAST is the Place that Anchors Strong Testimony."*

PUT THE PAST IN ITS PLACE

The people that throw your past in your face also have skeletons in their closets, and it's just easier for them to keep the focus on you because then the spotlight is not on them.

As new things come up, you can repeat this process as often as needed. Or as new aspects of something old surfaces you may return to this process so that these new discoveries don't become stumbling blocks.

After all, these are the things that we hold on to, the things we let build and cause us to give more attention to what's behind us than we do to what lies ahead of us. Doing this exercise will help you put your past in its proper place and perspective, and assist you in redirecting your attention, energy and power towards what you desire to be, do and have. If you desire to live your purpose, I encourage you to make this exercise a practice and remember this, our past is never just about us. It is also for those who are meant to be touched by us.

CHAPTER 7

No Strangers on the Journey

Smile at strangers and you just might change a life.
– Steve Maraboli

O ver the span of our lifetime many people will cross our paths. There will be people you'll want desperately to forget. I understand. I've got those too. Then there will be others who will leave a lasting pleasant memory. In either case, every person in every situation has a place and purpose in your life. I don't believe in coincidences. Things don't just happen.

In 2016, I attended a conference in Atlanta. I was part of a Facebook group for the conference and there was a lot of buzz and excitement leading up to the conference. We were so connected in this group after years of following this inspirational speaker. It truly felt like a community, as many of us were seeking to find our passion and step into a new level of boldness to do it. We were encouraged by the conference sponsors to find people in the group to room with to save on the costs. I happened to know one of the sisters in the group, Shereese, from another event so we decided to join forces and find two other women to room with. We did just that. Shereese and I were from Maryland, April was from Massachusetts and Celeste was from Nebraska. We planned all the logistics through phone calls and texts prior to the conference. Now, you may be scratching your head and thinking that four women, practically strangers, sharing a room sounds like a Molotov cocktail!

Nope. Actually, it was one of the most amazing experiences of my life. When we all got to the room and had a chance to talk face to face, it was like old college friends who hadn't seen each other since graduation. We talked about our families, our challenges, what led us to the conference, what we were expecting. We shared the emotions and excitement of the conference experience together and supported and encouraged one another. We ate and took pictures together. Laughed and cried together. We marveled at how genuine the bond was between us and how truly blessed we were to be sharing these moments.

ARE YOU KIDDING ME?

The jaw-dropping moment came when Celeste and I were walking out of a session on the second day of the conference. We were having casual conversation and I mentioned something about Periscope, one of the social media platforms that I was using at the time to connect with people all over the world.

She grabbed my hand and stopped us in our tracks. She looked at my nametag, which had my name and company name, TruSynergy, LLC on it, then looked back at me. She let out a loud gasp and said, "Wait a minute! TruSynergy! You're the TruSynergy that I've been following on Periscope? You mean you and I have been talking for the last six months, halfway across the nation, and we end up in Atlanta sharing a room together, not even realizing we had a connection already!" We screamed and hollered all the way to our room. And I will never forget what she did after we shared our discovery with our other roommates. Celeste fell to her knees and began to pray. She thanked the Creator for divinely bringing us together and gave thanks for whatever was to come as a result of our meeting. To this day we are still in touch, and brainstorming about ways we can collaborate that will give me a good reason to travel to Nebraska. Even as I write this, I am still in awe of how the Creator divinely leads us to those with whom we are meant to connect.

EVERY INTERACTION COUNTS

Everyone and everything play a role in our lives, even those people and experiences that don't bring a smile to our faces at the thought of them. Even the most tumultuous and painful relationships teach us something about who we are, and more importantly, help us to grow into who we were created to be, IF we see it that way.

There are instances when someone puts in a good word for us regarding a job we desire. People mentor us, formally and informally. Another person may introduce us to someone that becomes a great resource and a setup for something amazing to happen for us. It may not be evident as things are occurring how those relationships or circumstances will impact our lives, but if we ask for wisdom

63

it will be revealed in due time. So, what does all of this have to do with your purpose? EVERYTHING!

Do you get that even the most annoying person and trying incident fits into your destiny? I often think about the people I've encountered, especially in my corporate experience, that have challenged me. The spectrum of experiences is quite wide, as I'm sure they are for you. I've worked for managers who were knowledgeable and well respected, who challenged me to follow their example. I've had coworkers and colleagues who have become lasting friends. I've also had less than exciting or memorable experiences, yet they were equally significant. I think about those who were so used to doing things a certain way, not willing to budge from the proverbial "we've always done it this way." When I would ask questions or bring new ideas to the table, it was not always well received.

I've also had those who, in conversation, forgot that I too was an adult and not their 5-year-old child. You know how those conversations go because I'm sure you've had many of them. They're conversations with people that try to make you feel like you're not good enough because you don't do things like they do, or you haven't been connected with what they do long enough to know how things work.

TUG OF WAR

I remember one encounter with a coworker at a meeting to discuss a project. We were charged with collaborating on how to simplify processes that we both worked on. It was one of those projects that I knew would take some adjusting and require us to work together as a team. It was also one that I didn't look forward to because I had minor clashes with this person before. From the outset, the tension in the room was thick. It felt much like a game of tug-of-war. Every idea that I suggested there was a counter argument for why it wouldn't work. It became quite clear that I was up against a major challenge. I could feel heat coursing through my body and the hair rising up on the back of my neck. My first instinct was to lash out because I felt like I was being attacked. I realized, however, that this wasn't so much about how I could get this person to be open to new ways of doing things, it was about me keeping myself in the right flow of energy while we played this game.

> When we observe the behavior of
> others we get to choose what we want
> to emulate, what we ought to ignore and
> how we get to act and decide what kind
> of example we'd like to be for others.

Sometimes we feel negative vibes and witness adults behave like little children when they don't get their way. We might think incidents like these are about what's going on in that space and time, but it's bigger than that. Situations like these and the people we encounter in them are there for a reason and it's not just to solve the issues on the table. Rather, it's about forcing you to dig deep within you to decide who you'll be regardless of how they choose to show up. When they go low will you take the high road, or will you sink to their level? See, "No Strangers on the Journey" isn't just about the casual, fleeting encounters. Actually it's about the people who are in your wagon that you have to travel with, even if for a brief time—the ones you'd much rather ditch on the side of the road rather than go any farther with. This was one of those moments for me. At one point I just sat quietly and stared at the person. I was in shock and disbelief at her behavior. I carefully considered my response because I wanted it to be one that would expand and grow me, one in which I would maintain my integrity and rise above the fray. Oh, and yeah, I wanted to keep my job! I intended to win this game of tug-of-war. The only way I could do that was to speak in a calm, direct manner. If I could do that then I'd be fine with however the cookie crumbled. See, I recognized that this person was a test; she came to help me appreciate how thick my skin was. If I'd lashed out and behaved badly too I would have failed the test.

But if my response was a smart move then I would pass. That time I passed. I can think of many other instances where I failed because I allowed other people's behavior to dictate how I showed up, rather than forcing or inspiring them (and myself) to rise to a higher level. I can recall plenty of instances where a conversation or act caused me to forget that I was an adult. Those too were part of the journey for they helped to build my character.

GROWING PAINS

Have you ever desired to release some weight? When you start working out at the gym your first couple of days don't feel so good, right? You're sore the next morning, maybe quite a few mornings your muscles ache. But if you

66

hang in there, keep hitting the gym no matter the pain your muscles get stronger and the pain lessens.

The same is true with the coworker, family member, or friend who tries your patience, hurts you or makes you angry. Learning how to handle people, more importantly yourself, in difficult situations grows you. If that's going to happen we have to be in tune with how we are feeling around certain people, call it out and then reverse it. For example, for years I felt intimidated when I was around certain people because it appeared they knew more than me. I would sit in meetings listening to these people speak so intelligently about technical things that I really had no interest in. Still, I felt inferior because I didn't know how to speak their language. What I didn't realize was that telling myself "I feel intimidated" generated feelings of inadequacy, of not measuring up, fear, and even low self-esteem. These emotions were all too familiar. They took me back to my youth. It's amazing how much of a mark those experiences left on my life. So there are always two principles at work: recognizing the emotions attached to other people and reversing that affect. Reversing that affect meant I had to turn it around by affirming that I brought just as much value as others did.

In these instances, the people and situations that challenged me were a part of my evolution. Why? Because they were being used to show me something about myself, who I am, and what I'm made of. What I now know is that many of the people I worked with in corporate America helped me a great deal, beyond pushing papers and getting assignments done. These "strangers" taught me enough about myself for me to get that I didn't want to do what they were doing for the rest of my life. This doesn't take anything away from them. As a matter of fact, those tough times tested and strengthened me and pushed me closer to my purpose.

OH NO HE DIDN'T!

Years ago I was asked to coordinate a friend's wedding. She opted to have a minister from her home state of New York to officiate the ceremony. No problem. I'd coordinated many ceremonies before and worked well with wedding parties and families; so it was all good. The minister was late for the wedding rehearsal the night before and only had a few words to say when he finally did arrive.

On the day of the wedding, the bride had given me specific instructions that I needed to get to the minister so he would know what her wishes were. I don't remember exactly what the request was, but I know it was something we forgot to mention the night before. So I wrote a note and asked one of the hostesses to deliver it to the minister, because I was taking care of other matters. The ceremony went on without a hitch! Everyone was so happy and excited at the joyful union they'd just witnessed. I was happy too because I saw hard work coming together to make something beautiful. As I walked up to the pulpit to start getting things ready for picture taking I was confronted by the minister, who I thought was about to compliment on what a beautiful job I'd done. Instead, he put his finger in my face and snapped, "I am a professional! Don't you ever send me a note with instructions on what to do during a ceremony!" I stood there in shock. Not only was this man a minister but he'd stuck his finger in my face. I was livid. I thought to myself, "What a coward. Not only does he think it's okay to do what he did, but he then runs off and leaves me no opportunity to respond."

Or so he thought. Like a peacock, in my finest gray two-piece suit and duster jacket I swiftly went after him. I could feel the heat rising up the back of my neck; it felt like I was about to boil over. I wanted to spit, cuss, scream and kick ass. Yes, the minister's ass!

When I reached him, I said, "Excuse me, but don't you EVER put your finger in my face again, you so-called minister! Then just walk away! What kind of minister are you? What if I was someone who was troubled and needed some direction? Would your cowardly actions get me closer to the God you claim to serve?"

After I finished, he turned and walked out the door mumbling something under his breath. I could not believe what had just happened. I didn't tell the bride and groom or their family, until later. I wanted them to know that I was planning to write a letter about the incident and send it to the minister's church overseer. And I did just that.

I never received a response and, to this day, I don't know what, if anything, ever happened to that minister.

But what I do know is that that was a time when I decided I was not going to be disrespected. In that moment I wasn't the little girl afraid to speak up for herself or the foolish adolescent who was going to keep quiet when her boundaries had been crossed. Though he really made me angry, I believe he and that incident were sent my way to show me how powerful I am. This is something I hold on to when the little voice in my head tries to tell me otherwise.

GET YOUR WORKOUT

I'm sure you can think of your own experiences where you've had to decide whether to absorb negative vibes and emotions from others or remain true to the positive energy within you. These are moments of choice and we constantly have to make them.

We have the opportunity to rise higher and allow others to stay small if they so choose. Not in an arrogant or superior way, but in a way that says we are determined to hold on to our own power. It often takes months, even years, of encounters with some people for us to know when to detach from them. Returning to the gym analogy, regular workouts strengthen our physical bodies.

Likewise, our connection with abrasive people and challenging situations strengthen our resolve. We learn to use our affirmative power to focus on exactly who we are and what we bring to the table. Moreover, people serve their purpose by making us self-evaluate. This is one of the keys to living your purpose because the wrong attitude in these situations can keep you from living your full potential. I can't think of anyone who doesn't have to deal with people, no matter what their purpose. So every encounter is like getting a good workout!

Some people come into our life to lead
us to the next stop on our journey.

70

GAME CHANGER

The same is true for those people that we have a good relationship with. I'll never forget the day I met one of my close friends and business partners, Myra Jackson. It was 2013, the Monday after the Baltimore Ravens won the Super Bowl. By this time I was gone from my employer of nineteen years and working for another reputable company. On this day, I was sitting at my desk waiting for Myra to meet with me for some one-on-one time.

She was new to the company and I was responsible for showing her what I did in my job. That morning she walked over to my desk with a beautiful smile that looked like a ray of sunshine. She wore a purple blouse. I immediately identified with that because I was still on cloud nine from the Ravens win. In fact, I was sporting my purple victory color as well. We instantly hit it off. After all the formal business talk, the conversation turned into 20 to 30 more minutes of talking about all the things that mattered to us—our children and a bigger, brighter future for ourselves. We discovered we had so much in common when it came to family, goals, health and wellness, and she spoke highly of a friend that she thought I should connect with because she was doing things that were aligned with my passion for helping people to live well mentally, physically and spiritually. Weeks later Myra introduced me to a business opportunity that was a good fit for me because it complemented everything I was doing outside of my nine-to-five. In the past, I never saw myself in this type of business but I was excited about it and it made so much sense that I couldn't say no.

Connecting with Myra was a blessing in so many ways. From her I learned the value of not holding on to what happened yesterday, to live in the now and dream big for the future—confirmation for where I was at that point in my life. I added another jewel to my bag of genuine friendships where unconditional love and respect were the cornerstones. My relationship with Myra powerfully speaks to the truth that there really are no strangers on the journey. See, I had only been on the job a few months when Myra joined the company. Remember I'd worked for a company for nineteen years when I found myself needing to look for a new job. Suddenly I was in a strange place. I was in the market for a new job, an unfamiliar and scary place. Yet, I felt like I was in a necessary phase of my life and I honestly believed that being in this situation was the best thing that could have happened to me. If it were up to me, I would have stayed right where I was but the Creator knew that something needed to change. I needed to move because there were pieces of my purpose that I had to discover, and there was a new mindset I needed to help me embrace it. Myra was another key piece to his puzzle.

MORE THAN BUSINESS

That was so perfectly orchestrated. I was destined to meet her because she was an integral part of my future. Myra connected me to the business opportunity that allowed me to strengthen my presentation skills and set me on a path to financial freedom. She was the link to other successful people who would become coaches and mentors to me. Myra was the leader who exposed me to personal development that reinforced my faith and belief in myself. She was a friend that I could be real and authentic with. Our connection wasn't just about a great business opportunity, but it was about a philosophy of achievement rooted in the belief that anything is possible. A new friendship and many blessings came out of that one meeting, and there are even more successes on the horizon that we have yet to experience.

I think about the countless other friendships that have added value to my purpose and helped shape me, from long-time friends and family who have shown unconditional love and support to the casual acquaintances. I remember the time when I was hosting a coffee tasting at a gym and met a woman who invited me to a business networking meeting.

At the networking event I met a gentleman who was a cameraman for a local television station and also had his own studio.

He ended up producing several episodes of my TruWoman show, a YouTube series where I showcase the stories of dynamic women in the community. That experience gave me insight into what goes on behind the camera, helped me to become comfortable on the set with the teleprompter, and supported me in developing my interview skills as I connected with some amazing women. That was just the beginning. There's so much more to be done in that arena. That will come, and because I crossed paths with an experienced cameraman the foundation is already set for the next opportunity.

Smiles from strangers and hugs from
friends are good for the heart.

73

People serve their intended purpose in your life. Sometimes for a season, other times a lifetime. Strangely enough, very often we intuitively know what that time frame is for each person that crosses our path. Sometimes we don't.

AN ANGEL AND STRANGER

One day I was at the car wash. As I waited for my car to go through the tunnel a gentleman waited for his to come through as well. We started talking about the weather and having a clean car. He asked me what I did for a living. I told him about my passion to help people find their "TruSynergy," that place of harmony between mind, body and spirit. He said, "Wow, that sounds awesome. And you seem very confident and bold, so that sounds great." Now, we had never met before but that brief encounter did two things for me: First, it showed me how far I'd come in my journey of building self-confidence. Granted, I'm tall, I keep myself looking nice, I have degrees, certifications and licenses under my belt but the struggle with self-confidence was real. I know now that my challenges were rooted in what I shared with you about my painful past. But on that particular day not only did I exude a certain presence (and I don't say that arrogantly) but when I opened my mouth to speak about my passion; I felt good about what I was saying. It just flowed over my tongue with ease. Secondly, this encounter reminded me that my Creator, which I call God, will always send me what I need when I need it.

On that day, I felt like this man was sent to confirm that I can be bold and speak confidently about what matters to me and that boldness is what I will need to keep pressing forward into the things that are in store. I may never see that man again, and to be honest I can't even tell you what he looked like, but he was in my life for a brief but impactful moment. At that time, I could identify quickly why he crossed my path. Sometimes it's not as clear-cut, but as time goes on, as we leave ourselves open, we can connect the dots. So whether your encounters with people make you feel good or stretch you, recognize there really are no "just by chance moments" and there are no strangers on the journey.

PURPOSE PRINCIPLES

Who is it that has impacted your life? Take some time to make a list of ten people that have crossed your path and the value they've brought to you, even if it was someone that you didn't have a good experience with. There's value in those relationships too. This could be family members, friends, a major relationship or a casual acquaintance.

Maybe your encounter with them was as recent as yesterday or as distant as ten years ago. When you look at the people that have touched your life, I'm sure you'll see threads of love, anger, happiness, frustration, joy, hurt, and a myriad of other emotions engendered by each experience. All of these experiences were divinely orchestrated to help create you, the you that has lives to touch, a mission to complete, purpose to fulfill!

75

CHAPTER 8

Gratitude

Be thankful for what you have; you'll end up having more. If you concentrate on what you don't have, you will never, ever have enough.
— Oprah Winfrey

Through the ups and downs of my life's journey I've discovered one of the keys that is readily available to unlock new levels of grace in every situation, Gratitude. Until recently, I didn't realize just how powerful gratitude is. It's easy to be grateful when everything is going the way you want and you feel like you're on top of the world. When we see things line up for us this can fill us with joy and excitement. But the true test comes when you're in a place of uncertainty. When the world as you know it is turned upside down will you still be grateful? When your back is so far against the wall that you could disappear into it, can you still express gratitude? Yes, these are the times when gratitude can be hardest to access. It's like looking at hidden pictures. You know the pictures that have all sorts of objects hidden in plain sight, and you have to see how many of those objects you can find?

At first you just see all the obvious stuff, but when you look closely you start to notice things that were at first difficult to see because they blended so well into the rest of the picture. Once you find them, you realize just how easy they were to spot. Gratitude, in a sense, is like that. Many things come together to create the picture of your life. The bills, the relationships, the job, looking for a job, dealing with people on the job, frustrations, anger, hurt, disappointment—all come together to become your picture. Underneath all of it ought to be a well of gratitude. However, too often we get so busy with life that we forget to acknowledge the things for which we are grateful.

The beauty of gratitude is that all you need is you! You don't have to wait on anyone else to give you permission to express your gratefulness. Some may ask, "How can I be grateful when my husband just left me for another woman?" Another may insist, "How in the world can I be grateful when I don't even know how I'm going to pay my light bill?" Somebody else may complain, "I don't have anything to be grateful for, my life is a hot mess!"

Another person may say they have nothing to be grateful about when they get up every day to go to a job that doesn't excite, fulfill or make them feel valued. OK, all of these are valid questions and concerns. Here's the answer: Even during our darkest hours there is ALWAYS something to be grateful for and keeping that in perspective should always be at the forefront of our minds.

You can show gratitude in a multitude of ways, but like the hidden objects in those pictures it can take some energy and effort to find these things. We tend to focus so much on all the stuff that we don't want that we totally miss the hidden blessings and lessons worthy of gratitude.

FIND THE GOOD

Here's a case in point. Remember when I talked about feeling trapped working my nine-to-five job, knowing my heart yearned for something more for myself and my family? Some days it was tough to go to work because I couldn't stop thinking about how I was spending hours working for someone else's company, rather than using that time to advance my own dreams. This is where the lines of gratitude and complaint can become blurred if we're not careful.

Complaining would have kept me finding everything wrong with my job, while gratitude made me thankful that I *had* a job. I knew there were people in the unemployment line who would have slapped their best friend's mother for my job. Gratitude means finding the good in a situation even if it doesn't feel good to you at the time.

> God puts food on the table and makes a way out of no way.

There were many times when I was between pay periods, you know the living paycheck-to-paycheck saga that many of us endure. One time in particular, we desperately needed to get to the grocery store; but I wouldn't have any money until my payday. Lord knows that seemed like many moons away. Every day that week as I drove home from work I kept wondering what we were going to have for dinner. Now don't get me wrong, we had food in the cupboards. But it wasn't the kind of food that we really liked, and even that was getting extremely low. And we were missing all the extra stuff, and some of the necessities and staples.

I remember preparing dinner one night from things I didn't even realize I had—a bag of turkey meatballs from the freezer, gravy from the pantry, a block of cheddar cheese, a box of macaroni and a can of baked beans. I threw all of that together and voila, a gourmet meal! I can still recall the joy I felt as I cooked and whispered words of thanks. It wasn't a meal I would have planned (unless it was a cookout), but seeing the look on the kids faces and hearing them scream "Ooooh, macaroni and cheese!" made my heart swell with gratitude. The biggest expression of gratefulness came after everyone ate and had seconds and there were a few days worth of leftovers! As I was putting the food away I smiled and silently said "thank you God," for He had made a way out of no way. I could have complained and sang, "oh woe is me" because the cabinets and fridge were not overflowing. But I pulled together what I did have. When I got over what I didn't have I saw that I actually had more than enough.

THANK YOU

It sounds easy, right? Just be grateful. Give thanks and be joyful. The reality is that some days it was extremely hard because of financial burdens, not being satisfied in my professional career, trying to maintain my family and building a business were taxing too.

There were days when I could have created a mural with the piles of mail that I got. Come to think of it, that might have been a good way to deal with all the bills that, at times, I wasn't sure how I was going to pay. Even as I write this book, this is my reality. There have been nights when I'd fall asleep at the computer because I had just one more thing to do to get me one step closer to bringing my dreams to fruition. There were moments when I would scratch my head, sometimes cry, as I wondered how I was going to make it all work.

See, the vision is there and I know the kind of life I want for me and my family, but it hasn't all shaped up like the picture in my mind, at least not yet. Even still, despite all of that there's one thing that brings me out of despair: Gratitude. There it is again. Gratitude. It makes me say "thank you" when I open my eyes in the morning, before I put one foot on the floor because I'm blessed with another opportunity to keep pressing forward, regardless of how things look. Gratitude makes me say "thank you" as I walk to the bathroom to shower, brush my teeth, find clothes to wear and dress myself each day because I think about the person who couldn't do those things on her own.

Gratitude made me remember how I always got to where I needed to go even though there were times that I couldn't fill up the gas tank. Gratitude made me appreciate the still, quiet moments at the beach with friends and family even though I didn't have a lot of money. Still, I had so much.

> When we're grateful for the small
> things the Universe knows we can be
> trusted with its abundant supply.

SMALL THINGS MEAN SO MUCH

Let's face it, sometimes we're only grateful for the big things. I was elated when I received bonuses every March from a former employer. When I had a partial hysterectomy that alleviated excessive bleeding and there were no other health threats, I was singing praises. When we got approved for our first house my husband and I were on top of the world with excitement. Moving from one job to the next and experiencing no lapse in pay during the transition was a true blessing. All of these amazingly awesome things happened to me, and I was thankful for how they worked out in my favor. But big things don't necessarily happen every day. However, we can find gratitude in the smallest things all throughout the day. We must lean into this thought.

Doing so shifts us into a new mindset and opens us up to even more possibilities. Here's how. When you think on the things that you're grateful for, rather than focusing on the things that are not going so well, you automatically put your mind, body and spirit in a place of experiencing good.

It doesn't mean you're ignoring things that challenge you. It means you're making a conscious decision to allow the good to influence you and your perspective on life. This is like making daily deposits into your Bank of Well Being! The more deposits we make the more we have to withdraw. We keep some for ourselves, to make us feel good, and share some with others so that they enjoy the benefits of gratefulness too.

I keep a gratitude jar on the shelf in my office and make a conscious effort to write out the things I'm thankful for, drop them in the jar and then reflect on them at the end of the year. I saw a Facebook friend share this so I decided to adopt this as my practice too. I also ask my children to name one thing from their day that they're thankful for. At first, I'm sure they thought I was crazy and it was a silly thing to do. Now they have come to appreciate the exercise and the reason why it's important.

That makes me happy. This is an essential part of fulfilling your purpose because when you allow your challenges to control your emotions you are doomed to be distressed and depressed. These states of mind prevent you from seeing opportunities, connections, and resources, and keeps you closed to the things that can propel you forward.

> A few ready to receive is more meaningful than a room full of people who are disengaged.

THY WILL BE DONE

In November of 2015, I hosted my first women's retreat. My goal was to have forty women. As we got closer to the event the registrations just weren't coming in as I had hoped they would. I had a wonderful planning committee working through all the details with me and we were prepared to serve, but when I realized we were well below my target I felt discouraged. A natural, human emotion, right? I'll never forget what my good friend and planning partner, Adrienne, said to me during one of our meetings. We were discussing the numbers and she said, "You are not going to get discouraged. We are going to do this and whoever needs to be there will be there."

That was a moment of gratitude because I was working closely with someone who cared enough about me and my vision to give me the encouragement and energy I needed to keep moving forward. From that moment on I decided that even if I had just one woman registered for the retreat, I would service her the same as if I had a room full of women. I gave thanks for every new registration that came in. I gave thanks for Adrienne and Tonia, who helped me plan down to the last detail. I gave thanks for the divinely inspired material that I was led to put together for the retreat workshops.

A total of eight women showed up, including me! Tonia, my mom, and I arrived at the venue ahead of everyone else so we could prepare to greet the ladies as they checked in. When I tell you it was perfect, it was PERFECT!

Since there were eight of us, we were given a beautiful cottage style house, away from the main hotel area. Our food was right there in the cottage. It was quaint and intimate.

One of the smallest things that filled me with gratitude was that the dining table in the cottage sat eight people, the exact number of women participating, reminding me that the weekend was divinely orchestrated according to The Creator's plans, not mine. Not to mention the fact that it was 80 degrees in November! The breakthroughs that the women experienced during the workshops were amazing. I doubt that this would have happened with forty women in the room—for sure the level of intimacy would have been different. Gratitude. The food was absolutely delicious. Gratitude. The service was impeccable. Gratitude.

I breathed in the "feeling" of it all and was overwhelmed in a wonderful way. Gratitude opened up everything that happened during that retreat. Had I focused on the low number of registrations or been negligent in my planning because the numbers weren't where I wanted them to be, I would have missed the opportunity to serve in the capacity that I was led to, and I would have done the women who invested their time and money a huge disservice.

ATTITUDE OF GRATITUDE

When we take our eyes off what's going wrong and what's not happening and turn our attention to all the reasons to be grateful, then we send a signal to the Universe that we appreciate all the gifts that we have been given, both big and small. A constant state of gratitude is like a key that unlocks new levels of possibilities, because when we give thanks it not only demonstrates our gratefulness for the things in the present but it shows that we can be trusted with what's to come. To take it even further, it's not just enough to say we're grateful—we want to *feel* gratitude. I was ecstatic when I was able to pull a meal together with so little left in the refrigerator. I even chuckled at how it all came together!

So here's the gratitude challenge: for thirty days make a conscious effort to be in an attitude of gratitude. One way to go about this is to say "thank you" *before* you get out of bed each morning. It's not complicated. It's a simple acknowledgement that inspires you to embrace the gift of a brand new day—because it really is a gift. So often we do other things first thing in the morning. We grab our smartphones to check our social media accounts. We check our emails and calendars.

We turn on the news or tune in to our favorite radio show. While these things feel awfully necessary, they don't set us up for a fulfilling day. Your heartfelt gratitude—and I insist that you say it out of your mouth—helps you cultivate that "life is a glass half full" perspective. For example, if you encounter a rude driver on your way to work don't focus on the negative behavior of that person.

KNOW WHEN TO LET GO

Don't get me wrong, I'm not saying there will never be a time when shit happens and you want to blow off some steam. You are human. But you can release that emotion, instead of holding onto it and allow it to create unhealthy conditions for you and those around you. Even the ability to let go is something for which to be grateful.

Don't go to work and re-live that rude driver incident by talking about it to your co-workers. That creates a wave of negative energy that can keep you tied up in knots. Instead, express gratitude for making it to your destination safely and for keeping your cool along the way, that is, of course, if you kept your cool, LOL.

CHAPTER 9

Keep Pushing

The moment you want to quit is the
moment you need to keep pushing.
– Author Unknown

iscovering your purpose is the fun and exciting part of the journey, and living in it day after day will require you to push through a lot of stuff even when you want to stop or when others don't believe in you. This may be the most important thing to remember because once you figure out what your purpose is, you have to recognize that things won't be handed to you on a silver platter. In fact, you will be met with more opposition when you not only discover your purpose but also resolve to live it. I hope this doesn't immobilize you or cause you to shrink away from your passion. When I talk like this it's my hope that you'll feel a little tremor in your body as you read my words. That tremor is the lifeblood of playing big. That's what we feel when we take a leap.

That tremor came when I acquired my first coaching client, who also happened to be another roommate from the conference in Atlanta that I spoke about earlier. I told you, there truly are no strangers on the journey. After the conference she called me to inquire about one of my program that was posted on my website. After we talked I was excited and nervous because I was taking the leap by accepting her as a client. *I want you to know that there are negative forces within you that don't want you to go any further than where you are right now.* At that time, a million thoughts ran through my head when I was preparing to send her my contract. *I'm not ready. I'm not qualified. Maybe I should go back and tweak my material.* This was the negative self-talk that I'd wrestled with in the past and it would win. But I knew it was time. So I leapt. Not only did I get a client, but she became a repeat client. She said my knowledge and expertise have helped her to become her true self. That makes my heart truly glad!

SHOCK THE NAYSAYERS

Imagine yourself as the change agent that causes someone to experience major breakthroughs in situations that have held them hostage for years.

Like my client Stephanie, who said my Transformation Success Strategy Program "was the best gift I could have given myself" because she gained insight and awareness into herself that she was unable to attain in 47 years!

Think about the person that you'll uplift with a kind word. What about the program you'll create that will transform lives? The weight you'll release. The degree you'll get. Whatever it is for you, there is a tremendous call to action on your life. When you move you'll inspire your family, friends, circle and communities to stop settling for mediocrity, get unstuck and live in *their* purpose.

It sounds wonderful and exciting doesn't it? But know this, there will be people whom you know and love who won't support you, that won't celebrate you, or understand why you're doing the things you're doing—going to a meeting, doing conference calls, working weekends, launching and running a business that doesn't align with their idea of success. What will you do? Will you give up, or will you push through the negativity and ignore the naysayers.

That is, if someone tells you that it will never work will you give in to doubt or keep moving forward and show them what you're made of?

> What lies behind us and what
> lies ahead of us are small matters
> compared to what lies within us. And
> when we bring what is within us out
> into the world, miracles happen.
> — Ralph Waldo Emerson

REBUKE THE DEMON

It'll be easy to quit, or worse, never get started in the first place. Staying in your comfort zone appears to be a safe place to be, besides, it falls in line with what many others are doing. When you stay put you become a part of the crowd. You do what society expects you to do. When you step outside of that others may not see your dream or goal; they certainly won't feel your desire. You may hear things like: It won't work. You don't have the money for that. Who do you think you are, anyway? No one has ever been successful at that. You've been saying it will happen for years and it hasn't happened yet, why bother? Then the little demon of doubt begins to take up residence in your head and you start replaying all those questions over in your mind. If you're not careful you'll begin answering those questions in a way that causes you to shrink, or you'll exhaust yourself fighting doubt. I've experienced this firsthand.

I was having a conversation with someone about my partnership in a direct sales company. I joined it for a number of reasons: I loved the product, it complemented the mission of TruSynergy, the personal development was life-changing, and I saw the monetary potential in it. In the conversation, I was being challenged on every point. The comments and the energy were so negative; there was no hope of getting this person to be open to my perspective or to accept my reasons for being involved. I had to make a decision. I could expect one of a few things to occur: I could continue to impress upon this person the reasons why I decided to be a part of this business, with the hopes of convincing them to see things my way. Or I could walk away from the conversation feeling dejected and defeated, as I questioned myself and my decision to join this company. Finally, I could walk away feeling completely comfortable with my decision, and feel even more empowered to move onward. I chose door number three. That didn't mean, however, I wasn't hurt, upset, and even a little angry about the exchange. Those emotions flowed through my tears, and I remember saying to myself, "I will succeed."

LOVE THEM WHERE THEY ARE

This doesn't mean people don't care about or love you. It just means that their view is different than yours. Accept that as fact and keep moving forward. I tell my coaching clients to attach their intentions to their "why," the compelling reason that will keep them connected to and in action with their intentions. When you begin to live purpose-minded and you're driven to make that purpose your life, those close to you may not understand. And they may not be willing or be able to go on the journey with you. When we don't understand something what do we do? We become critical of that thing or person. With each encounter you will need to make a decision, and it will always be the same: do I give up or do I keep pushing? What you decide will be rooted in whom you're committed to pleasing and what you believe about you, your dreams, goals and your purpose. In that moment I didn't really care what the other person thought about my decision, I stood my ground and that felt good. That good feeling made the tears worth it. It was almost like fuel.

We can get trapped behind a roadblock
or find a creative way to get around it.

LESSON LEARNED

You can expect roadblocks and moments of weariness, but this is where you have to look beyond appearances, what people think, and even your own feelings. Faith in the Creator and belief in yourself will be your anchors when you're gripped with fear and doubt. I remember when I was just about sixty days away from launching my company in 2010. The invitations for the launch event were printed. They, along with other marketing materials, had my logo and company name on them and I was ready for the mass mailing. I was so excited! I was on my way home one day from picking up the invitations when I got a phone call from an attorney who said I was in danger of trademark infringement. The company name I had chosen belonged to someone else! I cannot describe the sinking feeling in my stomach. I thought I had done everything I needed to do to register my name but apparently I missed something. I couldn't get home fast enough to break down. As soon as I hit that door the tears came. I questioned myself and how this could be happening, literally, on the eve of mailing out my invitations. I was distraught, trying to figure out what I was going to do. I did some research and sure enough the attorney was right and I was wrong.

Then it hit me. I was given the opportunity to cry and wallow, then one of those gratitude moments that I spoke of earlier washed over me. "Ok, that's enough," some part of me said. The blessing was that the invitations had not gone out! In the flurry of frustration, anger and confusion I seized the moment to be thankful. So now I had to figure something out, fast. I didn't have time to waste because the launch was only weeks away. I was at a decision point: do I give up or do I keep pushing? Giving up would have been easy. All I had to do was quit while I was ahead and send a notice out to folks that everything was canceled. I decided to keep pushing! That night I started thinking about new names, scribbling thoughts and words on a piece of paper. I made a list of things that I needed to do, including figuring out all the paperwork, re-filing requirements, updating my website and re-ordering invitations. All of this required time and money, neither of which I had to spare but I had to bite the bullet. This time I decided to research the name I came up with on the United States Patent and Trademark Office (USPTO) registry. When I discovered the name I liked was not being used I decided to register a trademark so there would be no confusion about ownership.

The invitation designer was so gracious, she worked with me to reprint and when it was all said and done I was about two weeks behind the original date that I'd intended to get the invitations out. No worries though, because I still had the time I needed to finalize other plans leading up to the big day. Another moment of gratitude and a lesson learned. I wasn't as thorough as I should have been and it cost me time and money—but not enough of either to cause me to stop.

NEGATIVE SELF-TALK

The fork in the road that points to giving up or to keep pushing ahead isn't just influenced by the things and people around you. Indeed, the biggest obstacles are within; they come from the person you see in the mirror every day, the one you spend the most time with, you. We get in our own way because of how we think. It's as if there's a cage in our mind and we are the prisoner, trapped in negative thinking. Consequently, we speak negative. Before we know it we've convinced ourselves as to why we can't accomplish something, why it just won't work. Negative self-talk tempts you to give up because it knows that if you keep pushing you'll not only change your life, but you'll transform the lives of others in the process.

Negative self-talk is loud and persistent and it'll have you doubt your abilities and compare yourself to other people.

> Comparing yourself to others
> is violence to the self.

KNOW YOUR WORTH

I reconnected with an old graduate school classmate at that Atlanta conference. Since we were both from Maryland, we vowed to meet for dinner when we got back home. She is a successful coach and works closely with a successful celebrity, so I was eager to learn anything she was willing to share at dinner. Why? Because success leaves clues. She asked me what I charged for my coaching programs and when I told her she calmly said, "You're not charging enough." My explanation was filled with negative self-talk because I compared my accomplishments and experience to others.

Sure, seasoned professionals may command a different pay rate. But you mustn't foolishly undervalue your gifts. My former classmate told me that that was exactly what I was doing. She suggested that I instead focus on all that I brought to the table instead of sizing myself up against others and their credentials.

When I asked her to clarify, she simply took me back to my credentials—my degrees, years of experience in the corporate world, my client testimonials and my life's experiences, which all helped me relate to my clients, were worth far more than what I was asking for. It was a huge ah-ha! moment, and big shift for me. I realized that I was my own obstacle. Then she told me in a direct but delicate way, "I want you to raise your prices NOW!"

She gave me specific next steps and I followed them to the letter. When the time came to set the price on the program I created as a result of our meeting and advertise it the negative self-talk returned. It went something like this, *"I can't do that! What will people think? Who's going to pay me that much to coach them?* "Keep moving, keep pushing," I told myself. So I did it. Knees knocking, fingers trembling, but I did it. I raised my rates, and I've secured several new clients since then! If you listen to doubt and fear you'll throw in the towel and concede defeat, sometimes even before you start.

DO IT AFRAID

> There will be times when you
> have to work alone. Embrace
> the journey. Everything you need
> will show up in due time.

Then there are the times when you have to be willing to go it alone because you are moving forward while others seem to be standing still, or not keeping up with your pace. It doesn't mean you're right and they are wrong. It just means what's right for you is different from what's right for them, and that's okay. It also doesn't mean you won't ever need help. All of us need the support of others on our way to successfully reaching a goal. Going it alone just means you have to be willing to take action whether others support you or not.

One night I dreamed I was jogging on a dark path. I couldn't see much to the left or right of the path. Ahead, in the distance, I could see a man. I became frightened because I was alone on this dark road, and I wasn't sure who this man was or his intentions. As I got closer to him he began to point me in the direction I should go. My fear began to subside. I followed his direction and ended up in a room full of people. I sat down at a table with a bunch of other people, and then someone came out and began serving us food and drinks.

I had that dream about ten years ago, yet it and its clear message are etched in my mind. It was prophetic. Jogging on that dark road by myself symbolized those moments when I was more excited about my dreams than anyone else. It was like the times when I kept my vision private because I wanted to protect it (not a bad thing) and, truth be told, didn't want to defend it or have to help anyone else "think big" enough to believe it. That can be a lonely place. The fear that I felt when approaching that stranger was about my fear of the unknown, those "do it afraid" moments. Getting closer to the stranger only to receive helpful direction was about my relationship with the Creator and yielding to His guidance. When doing so, it puts me in a place where all that I need is provided.

Every one of us is able to do great things, to make a difference in the world. Some, however, won't discover this because they'll be too busy doing what everyone else is doing. Some will scratch the surface but when the doubters get in their ear, they'll let their dreams die a slow death. Then others will tap into their vision and break it wide open, while those who didn't believe watch in awe.

My hope is that you're the one who's ready. Ready to move in spite of the fear and doubt and step into your greatness, your destiny, your purpose!

How do you *Keep Pushing* in the face of adversity and uncertainty?

PURPOSE PRINCIPLES

- Make a DECISION! Decide that you are going to do IT, whatever IT is for you. Whether it's starting a business, writing a book, releasing weight, creating a program, launching a project, traveling the world, make a DECISION! Then start! And don't stop until you've done it!

- RECOGNIZE that opposition will come and try to derail you. Remember, what you have to offer will make a difference in your world, whether that world touches your family, friends, local or global community.

- Understand that everyone won't celebrate you, so you'll need to be your own CHEERLEADER.

- Stay FOCUSED on your mission and know that it's much bigger and formidable than the obstacles you face.

97

NOW I KNOW

It's been an amazing journey, and to think that it's just getting started is even more exciting! There are many things that have played a part in discovering my purpose. What I know for sure is that all of my ups and downs, tears and joy have brought me to this moment: I now know that my purpose is to inspire millions of people to find their truth so they can transform their lives and have an amazing impact on their world. This is living in your purpose, enjoying complete fulfillment. I recognize that I have a connection with people. Uplifting and encouraging them is what I would do for free but I also know it's okay for me to monetize my gift. I think that my love for the day spa experience allowed me to get in touch with the importance of mental, physical and spiritual well-being, something that has become the focus of my life and my coaching programs.

The painful parts of my past, adjusting my plan to that of the Creator's, the people that I've encountered, and learning to find gratitude in all things have helped to anchor this truth for me. Now I get to share the message of turning pain-points into possibilities and support people in embracing the difficult things that can make a difference to them and those around them.

And it is my sincere hope that you have found something in this book that will help you discover and passionately live your purpose.

ACKNOWLEDGEMENTS

Walter and all of my family and friends, thank you for your love, support, encouragement and believing in me.

DeBora M. Ricks, my book midwife, editor, and coach, I appreciate you for pushing me beyond my comfort zone and helping me to tap into my authentic voice.

ABOUT THE AUTHOR

Ericka Sallee, Speaker, Coach, and Author is the owner of TruSynergy, LLC, a personal coaching and professional development company that supports clients in becoming the best version of themselves. Ericka has a bachelor's degree in Psychology from Frostburg State University and a master's degree in Negotiation and Conflict Management from the University of Baltimore. She is passionate about empowering others to live their full potential, and has thus coined herself as the Tru' Transformation Success Coach. Ericka believes that when people find that truth they can transform their lives and impact their world. It is that passion that moved Ericka to create the YouTube series *The TruWoman Show*, which features dynamic women who have overcome tremendous odds to achieve success. Ericka uses this series, individual and group coaching programs, workshops, speaking engagements and social media outlets to encourage individuals to create their best life and live it to the fullest.

For the corporate client, she delivers stress management and effective communication trainings, and supports them in creating a corporate culture where every employee feels respected and valued and inspired. In her talks and trainings,

Ericka loves sharing simple principles and relatable stories that connects her to her audiences in a powerful way. Ericka lives in Maryland, enjoys self-care, traveling, movies, good food and wine, and spending time with family. Visit her at www.trusynergy.org. Send emails to trusynergy@comcast.net.